Praise for Lisa Parker and *Mu ... Moment*

"Lisa Parker is that rarest of breeds: an individual who has found her life's passion and pursues it daily with great energy and enthusiasm. Having been a client of Lisa's for many years, I read Managing the Moment *with elevated anticipation and interest. It is a singular work and is authentically Lisa; authoritative in its knowledge of and experience with the subject matter and unique in its presentation and insight. It is a must read for anyone who seeks to make a positive impression and maximize influence in their chosen arena."*

Dan Cappello
President and CEO, MEI, LLC

"What comes naturally to some leaders completely evades others. Why? Lisa Parker uses her years of executive coaching experience to get right down to the heart of the matter: facing the truth about one's leadership presence means managing behavior to inspire followership. Managing the Moment *is an honest view of how one's leadership style can positively or negatively shape a corporate culture."*

Patricia L. Glorioso
Head of Human Resources, The Rockefeller Group

"We all want to come across as confident, focused and engaging, but it's not always easy to pull that off, especially when we are in a stressed or low-energy state. Lisa Parker is right: we think we do a good job of hiding those bad days, but we fool ourselves. Managing the Moment *is a clearly written guide designed to lead the reader through self-examination, awareness, and action so that leaders can embrace and demonstrate their strengths with consistency and confidence."*

Adele Puhn, M.S., C.N.S.
author of The 5-Day Miracle Diet

"A great executive coach reveals insights about ourselves that enable us to make the most out of our leadership opportunities, and nobody does it better than Lisa Parker. Managing the Moment *persuasively argues that successful leaders require Presence with a capital P to stand apart, earn the respect of others and gain the influence they need to lead successfully. Parker offers great advice, compelling case studies, and insightful exercises that will help you hone your skills to best manage your moments and become a stronger leader.*"

Ed Keller
CEO, The Keller Fay Group;
author of The Face-to-Face Book and The Influentials

"Building executive presence is a regular topic in my development discussions with staff who have high career aspirations. I have turned to Lisa on many occasions to help members of my team improve their leadership style, their communication skills and their confidence, so it's terrific that she has put all that knowledge in a practical, actionable book that uses stories and case studies to make the big points. Managing the Moment *will be a real hit with leaders who want to build or strengthen their brand.*"

Christine Marcks
President, Prudential Retirement

"Parker hits the nail on the head in Managing the Moment. *In this engaging book on effective leadership style and presence, she manages to simply and honestly quantify the seemingly unquantifiable. In a humorous and pragmatic style, Parker explains what presence is and its criticality not only to personal executive success, but to the success of the enterprise. Her framing of presence in terms of personal branding is insightful. These concepts can be put to work straight away - a lively and eminently worthwhile read!*"

Elizabeth Lorenzini
Director, Business Operations,
Communications and Public Relations, Philips North America

"Managing the Moment *dissects the intricacies of presence by defining it, answering why you need it, and most important, how you can get it. The book's analysis of effective communication, building relationships and trust, and managing emotional triggers hits the mark on establishing a baseline for those needing to shape or reshape their leadership identity. How fortunate for us to now have a resource to pass on to everyone in the field of education, especially our emerging leaders.* Managing the Moment *is a top-shelf resource for me and my team."*

Dane Peters
Head of School, Brooklyn Heights Montessori School

"I approached Managing the Moment *with great interest, having been told at various times in my career that I possess this quality. The book offered me insights as to why others saw me as they did and offered some very practical suggestions as to how to further strengthen my presence. I had been under the impression that 'either you have it or you don't,' and was both surprised and encouraged that the attributes can be learned. I plan to buy the book for members of my academic leadership team for group discussion as to how we can empower ourselves and others to develop the attributes of presence."*

Harriet R. Feldman, PhD, RN, FAAN
Dean and Professor, College of Health Professions and Lienhard School of Nursing, Pace University

"Managing the Moment *does successfully what few other books relating to leadership qualities even attempt: it provides a clear and focused understanding of a quality – presence – that seems too ephemeral and too abstract to ever fully communicate let alone comprehend. Ms. Parker makes the vaporous quality tangible. She does not dumb-down the concept of 'presence' or diminish its idealized state or trivialize it by trying to reduce it to some easy-to-swallow idea. Rather, she carefully defines and makes accessible the reality of 'presence' for anyone. Readers will gain a great deal from this book and its thoughtful and instantly applicable insights. It should be a welcome presence on many an executive bookshelf."*

Denis Boyles
Author, The Modern Man's Guide to Life

MANAGING

the

MOMENT

MANAGING
the
MOMENT

A Leader's Guide to
Building Executive Presence
One Interaction at a Time

• LISA PARKER •

Published by Advantage, Charleston, South Carolina.
Member of Advantage Media Group.

ADVANTAGE is a registered trademark and the Advantage colophon is a trademark of Advantage Media Group, Inc.

Printed in the United States of America.

ISBN: 978-159932-393-0
LCCN: 2013933917

This publication is designed to provide accurate and authoritative information in regard to the subject matter covered. It is sold with the understanding that the publisher is not engaged in rendering legal, accounting, or other professional services. If legal advice or other expert assistance is required, the services of a competent professional person should be sought.

Advantage Media Group is proud to be a part of the Tree Neutral® program. Tree Neutral offsets the number of trees consumed in the production and printing of this book by taking proactive steps such as planting trees in direct proportion to the number of trees used to print books. To learn more about Tree Neutral, please visit www.treeneutral.com. To learn more about Advantage's commitment to being a responsible steward of the environment, please visit www.advantagefamily.com/green

Advantage Media Group is a publisher of business, self-improvement, and professional development books and online learning. We help entrepreneurs, business leaders, and professionals share their Stories, Passion, and Knowledge to help others Learn & Grow. Do you have a manuscript or book idea that you would like us to consider for publishing? Please visit advantagefamily.com or call 1.866.775.1696.

For my clients, who trust me with
their transformational moments,

and for my husband Craig, who always
remembers the moments that really matter.

———————————◆———————————

TABLE OF CONTENTS

INTRODUCTION

Why Are You Here?

Why Are You Reading This Book?

- ❏ You've gotten some feedback that you should "work on your presence" and you don't know what that means.

- ❏ You've been told you have excellent presence and you should continue to leverage it and you don't know what *that* means.

- ❏ A colleague described one of the senior partners as having "a certain presence" but couldn't tell you why she felt that way, and now you want to know more.

- ❏ You believe that having "executive presence" will benefit your career but aren't sure how to cultivate it.

- ❏ You've observed or experienced "mismanaged moments" and were intrigued by this book's title.

- ❏ You simply want to know if you *have* presence—or not.

If you checked off one or more of the boxes above, welcome! This book is for you.

At Heads Up Coaching, we believe that executive presence can be learned. Since 2007 we have trained over one thousand of executives and expanded our repertoire to include live and virtual programs for new managers and high potentials, special interest groups such as women's networks, and private coaching. This book is the result of our work with the dedicated business professionals who come to our seminars or seek coaching in order to understand and build their presence. They want to know:

- *What* is presence?

- *Why* do I need it?

- *How* do I get it?

Throughout this book, we will explore the relationship between effective leadership and one's style and presence. We will also investigate the impact that a leader's presence has on how people feel at work and subsequently on their levels of productivity and engagement.[1] You'll see that the reason to strengthen your presence is not just about you; it's about your team, your relationships, and the health of your business.

How to Use This Book

Like many of you, when I have a problem to solve, I want a practical solution that I can apply right now. You'll be glad to know that this book is chock full of practical tools you can use right now. This is not "touchy-feely, earthy-crunchy-granola" stuff, as we used to say in the '70s. This is practical skill building that anyone can do. Anyone. You may have tried to work on some aspect of your "style" or your presence before and failed, and decided that some people "have it" and some people don't, and you never will. That would be true if presence was some mystical quality. But it's not. It's real, it's behavioral, and it's within your grasp. So if you are committed to being the best that you can be, and if you are willing to do the work, then you can create the presence that you want to create. Yes, there are folks out there saying that presence cannot be taught. Baloney. We teach it every day and have done so for years with practical techniques that work. You'll have a chance to learn and practice many of these proven techniques as you move through the book.

- Every chapter will introduce you to one or more of the components of presence included in our presence model. Each component is behavior based and deeply informed by the elements of emotional intelligence. There are numerous activities in which you can make notes and apply the concepts to your own reality.

- Every chapter starts with a story. The case study stories at the beginning of each chapter and sprinkled throughout the chapters are all true. The names and identifying details are changed, and sometimes I've merged several people with similar challenges, but all of the stories are based on real people. You will meet successful business professionals struggling with challenges that will seem very familiar to you, either because you've faced that very same challenge yourself or because you work with someone who can't seem to crack the code and change his or her unproductive behaviors. In many places I will invite you to be the coach and to suggest a course of action for the person in the case study.

● Throughout the book, I'll pose questions to engage your imagination and stimulate your thinking. I encourage you to write all over it and make it your own.

● Please note: Gender-specific pronouns are always tricky. For the purpose of readability, I will use his/her and she/he interchangeably in this book. Except where specifically noted, the gender of the pronoun is not intended to suggest an issue is specific to any gender.

I look forward to taking this journey with you.

Lisa Parker
www.headsupcoach.com
December 2021

1

WHAT IS PRESENCE?

Jessica was exhausted as she trudged through the now-empty hallways, briefcase bulging with unfinished memos and reports. She made her way to the parking garage across the street where, once again, she was unable to fully open the driver's side door because of a massive SUV parked too close to the edge of the narrow parking space. In fact, its big, fat, dumb tires were right on the line. She scrawled a sarcastic note about how size matters and left it on the SUV wind-shield. Then she crawled in through the passenger side of her car, hastily cranked up the engine, and wound her way out of the garage and onto the darkened streets toward home.

◆

Mark was totally fed up with the lack of execution shown by the project team. Not only was the project three weeks late and grossly over budget, but the people on the team didn't seem to give a damn about the delays and overruns. He felt his temper building as he sat through yet another hour in the windowless conference room, listening to excuse after excuse. The satellite team on the phone wasn't helping either. The speaker on one of the phones kept cutting in and out, and every other sentence was "Sorry, could you repeat that? We couldn't hear the whole thing." After the tenth time, Mark yanked the phone cord out of the wall and snapped "There! That takes care of the bad phone lines! At least we accomplished one thing at this meeting!"

◆

Understandable? Totally. If you've spent any time in corporate America in the past twenty years these scenarios are so familiar that you're probably wondering if I've been spying on you (I have). What happened with Jessica and Mark is understandable, but it's not good, not good for them, not good for their colleagues, and not good for their companies. Jessica has no idea who owns that SUV. It could belong to someone in her department or someone she'll never meet, but she spent no time thinking that her note might have consequences. Mark's angry outburst is even worse. He's well known and in a position of authority. Guess how quickly the story of that yanked-out phone cord will spread?

We call these "moments of personal regret", moments we look back on and say, "Why did I do that?" or "I wasn't myself," or even "I lost my mind for a moment!" and we usually wish we could turn back the clock or get a "do-over" so we could make a different choice.

Managing those moments means making choices or, more specifically, making some choices and decisions in advance of the stressful or crisis moment so that we have more control when those moments occur. When we make deliberate decisions about how we want to behave in certain situations, we are actively managing our presence.

To Begin, What Is Presence?

When I pose this question at the start of my professional presence seminars, people often say:

- "It's how people perceive you."

- "It's that indefinable something that some people have, like charisma."

- "It's the first impression you make."

- "It's how you come across to other people."

- "It's your reputation, in a way."

- "It's the way you dress and your appearance."

These are good answers. How do they compare to the dictionary definitions below?

---

pres • ence /ˈprezəns/   Adapted from Dictionary.com

Noun:

1. The state or fact of being present, as with others or in a place.

2. The ability to project a sense of ease, poise, or self-assurance, esp. the quality or manner of a person's bearing before an audience: *The speaker had a good deal of stage presence.*

3. Personal appearance or bearing, esp. of a dignified or imposing kind: *A man of fine presence.*

4. A person, esp. of noteworthy appearance or compelling personality: *She is a real presence at these meetings.*

You probably noticed that points 2, 3, and 4 are very similar to those mentioned by our participants. It is very rare that someone mentions point 1 as her goal (though it is a very worthwhile goal that we will cover in Chapter Seven.) The other three get mentioned more often because they are the obvious outward signs of presence, and they seem as if they actually can be learned and managed. It's the reason people take our seminars, or buy this book. They see the impact of a leader with presence and they want to understand "the magic" so they can have a positive impact too.

So, presence is a noun, but it is not "a thing." Presence is many things. This leads us to the first premise of this book:

PREMISE #1

Presence Is the Sum of One's Actions and Behaviors

Actions and behaviors are the visible manifestations of your presence. It's what "they" see and hear when you're around. They notice one thing, and then another thing, and eventually they start to connect the dots to form a picture, just as we did in those children's activity books from years ago. But this is not child's play, not when your career is at stake. In the grown-up world, each dot represents information. Thus:

- ➲ Every moment in your day is like a point on a graph. It is a "data point" like those shown on the charts on page 21.

- ➲ People will connect those points or moments to try to find the pattern. Humans are hard-wired to find the patterns[3] and they get their data directly from you and indirectly from what other people say about you.

➲ You can influence what they think and say because you control the data that you put out there.

For example, imagine the leaders in both Figures 1 and 2 below are experienced, technically adept professionals with several years of employment in the company. You have had numerous interactions with each leader over time. Let's assume the horizontal axis is measuring a long time period —say six to twelve months—and the vertical axis is measuring the intensity of the interaction from your point of view. The star is a positive interaction, and the black triangle is a negative interaction, again from your point of view.

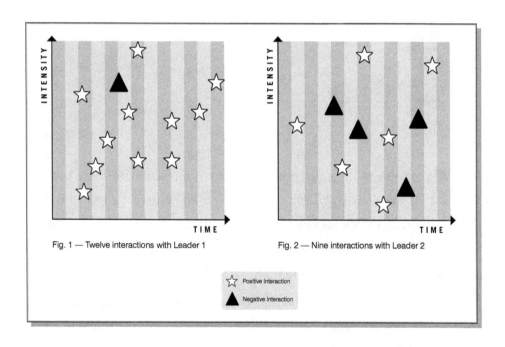

Fig. 1 — Twelve interactions with Leader 1   Fig. 2 — Nine interactions with Leader 2

☆ Positive Interaction
▲ Negative Interaction

WHAT DO YOU THINK?

What is your overall sense of Leader 1? Based on the pattern of your interactions with Leader 1, how might you characterize that one negative interaction?

_____

_____

_____

_____

Based on your interactions with Leader 2, how would you interpret that pattern of data points?

_____

_____

_____

_____

When we show these diagrams to people in our seminars, some have said, "I like Leader 1." Or, "I don't even know these people, but I would rather work for Leader 1 than Leader 2." And other folks have said, "I don't like Leader 2. I don't trust that person." How can people make these declarations about someone they've never met?

Easy. Once again, it's because of our desire for predictability, and Leader 2 is unpredictable. You never know what you are going to get with someone like Leader 2 and that is very stressful. Moreover, people likely experience Leader 2 in very different ways, and so they talk about that leader in very different ways. This means that Leader 2 does not have a very solid brand inside the company. Leader 2 is seen as "all over the place" or "uneven," which is not something most of us aspire to. And who is responsible for this scattershot reputation? Leader 2 is responsible. Leaders who behave in noticeable but inconsistent ways are either unaware of or unconcerned with how they come across, and so they do not actively "manage the moment" of each interaction. Thus they have a presence that is at best rather vague and diffuse, and at worst uncomfortable and untrustworthy.

Why do we like Leader 1? Leader 1 is more positive, yes, but Leader 1 is also more predictable, a trait most people appreciate. Most likely it is relatively easy to describe Leader 1's presence, and because of that consistency, people likely agree on their interpretation of Leader 1's behavior. Not only does this solidify Leader 1's internal brand, but—as you'll see in the true-life anecdotes in Chapter Six of this book—executives like Leader 1 can more easily recover from a bad day. In other words, because Leader 1 manages most moments, the one regrettable moment, however intense it is, is unlikely to destroy people's overall favorable perception.

Why Do I Need Presence?

Surely the answer to this question is becoming clear to you by now. Here's more:

> Picture this scenario: You and a friendly colleague are leaving a stressful meeting, and she says to you, "You seemed very tense in there ... you snapped at a few people ... did you realize that?" And you didn't.

> Or this scenario: You notice that a verbose, disorganized associate has put himself on your calendar for 5:00 PM,

and you groan to yourself, "I'll never get home on time tonight; doesn't he know he's a windbag?" And he doesn't.

What you don't know *can* hurt you. In both scenarios, the person is not aware of how he or she comes across to others, an essential component of building and managing one's professional presence. And just like Leader 1 and Leader 2, we need to manage all the moments to ensure that people perceive us in the way we want to be perceived.

And Finally, How Do I Get Presence?

So far, I haven't met anyone who was born knowing how to drive a car or sink the perfect putt. Every skill we have is something we had to learn, strengthen, and sustain.

PREMISE #2:

Behavior Can Be Learned (or Relearned)
and Actions Can Be Managed

Let's do the math: If "presence is the sum of our actions and behaviors" and if "behaviors can be learned," it follows that "presence can be learned." This is good news for you and for me: good for you because it is an achievable task, and good for me because I'm in the presence business!

Yes, it's true that some people are born with that certain something that makes people notice them, but this is not necessarily presence. Similarly, not everyone with presence was born with it. Far from it. Most of us have had to learn it one skill at a time, the same way we learned how to be a good manager, leader, or parent.

Let me warn you now: the "how" is the hard part.

For example, do any of these real statements sound familiar to you?

- "I've given Bob this same feedback for two years in a row during his performance review, and he says he will work on it, but nothing changes."

- "I know I talk too fast. It's the big joke in our family, and people ask me all the time to slow down, but it's just the way I am."

- "It drives me crazy the way she says 'like' all the time. I've pointed it out to her, but she still does it."

- "I've always had a soft voice. I know I should speak up but…"

Professional coach and author Alan Fine says, "the biggest obstacle in performance isn't 'not knowing' what to do; it's 'not doing' what we know."[4] Isn't that the truth? I *know* I should exercise more frequently, but I don't always *do* it. You probably have something that you know you should do, such as exercise, or not do, like smoke, and even knowing that isn't enough. The same is true with trying to strengthen your presence. You might know what presence is and why it matters, and you've gotten feedback from your manager that you have to work on it, and you want to work on it, but things get busy and you forget and slip back to your old ways. It happens, even with the best intentions.

Why is that?

It's because much of our behavior is ingrained and even unconscious. You can't just know you have to make a change, you have to *do* something about it. It's the doing that makes it stick. It takes a great deal of repetition, practice, and feedback to successfully replace an old habit with a new one. This too has to do with the way our brains are wired. Any time we try new behavior, it feels odd and uncomfortable. Sometimes the discomfort alone is enough to stop us, but it's very important to press on. People who are extremely anxious when making presentations tell us they feel less anxious when they have the chance to present more often and when they actually set aside the time to practice. Yale neuroscientist Amy Arnsten confirms the science behind that. Says Arnsten: "Practice and habit help override the mental shutdown that occurs when we are anxious."[5] So keep in mind that working on your presence means changing behavior, and that means...practice.

The Three Little Words I Love to Hear

No, it's not what you think. My favorite three little words are:

"Up Until Now ... "

As in:

- *Up until now,* I've always seen my superfast talking as a part of my high-energy style. But now, I realize that it puts a barrier between me and other people because they can't understand me, so I'm working to slow down my speech.

- *Up until now,* I spoke softly because I dislike it when people are overly loud. But now I understand that if people have to work too hard to hear me, they may tune me out completely, so I'm working to find a volume level that is loud enough without being overbearing.

The great thing about "up until now" is that it passes no judgment about "then." It assumes that we developed certain habits for very good reasons. Those behaviors worked for us back then. But now those same behaviors are getting in the way of what we want to accomplish. So now we start anew, making choices that suit our goals and aspirations and further our professional presence. If your career is worth working on, your presence is worth working on.

PREMISE #3:

Your Career Is a Collection of Moments

We tend to remember our big "capital M" Moments, such as that Moment you learned you were going to be named vice president, or that Moment someone on your team said you were the best boss she'd ever had. But what do *they* remember? When they talk about you (of course they talk about you!) what Moments come into their minds? Is there a thoughtless note or dangling phone cord in your past? How about a forwarded e-mail with a careless remark? A voice message left in anger? An impatient comment for the cafeteria cashier?

THE TAKEAWAY:

- A collection of moments is a collection of data points.

- People will connect the points in the way that makes sense to them. They will then watch for evidence that supports the pattern ... and they will find it.

- Thus, your pattern becomes *their truth about you.*

The truth about you can be a good thing: it allows people to forgive and even forget the rare moments of regret. Or it can be a bad thing, causing people to attribute regrettable moments to a "difficult person" reputation that is tough to shake.

Purists dislike it when I use the word "truth" the way that I did in the box, but research has shown that once human beings make up their minds about something, it is very hard to change their opinions. Thus the first impression you give, when connected to other data, is very true—*to them.*

As difficult as it is to change people's minds, you still have the power to shape people's opinions about you. *You* decide how you want to be perceived. *You* decide how you want to be known. *You* determine your own professional presence. And that's good news, because this book will help you get there.

PREMISE #4:

We May Not Know What Presence Is, but We Know It When We See it

For example:

⮑ Jake is the General Manager of a big box retail store. He told me about a time where he was chatting in the aisle with his boss's boss, a very tall man and the group's VP, when a new associate walked behind the VP and mimed to Jake, "Wow! Who's that?"

⮑ Alaina walked her employee Leo upstairs to meet their new boss, who was recently hired away from the competition with great fanfare. Leo was skeptical. He admired Alaina and thought she should have gotten the top job. Alaina smiled and said, "Just wait until you meet her." After the brief meeting Leo turned to Alaina and said, "Wow! Now I get it."

⮑ It was my first week in a new job at a big corporation and it happened to be the week of divisional "town hall" meetings. I listened to speaker after speaker, most of them still unknown to me. When one speaker in particular delivered his speech, I was completely captivated. I turned to my new boss and said, "Wow! Who's that?"

The three leaders in these examples obviously have presence, but why? What was that "wow" factor? What are these leaders doing that makes them stand out from the others? Can anyone do it? Can you do it?

Yes. By studying what these and other captivating leaders do, you can begin to understand what presence is and how to have it yourself.

ACTIVITY

Let's start by noticing what is special about people with presence. Here's an activity that I do in my workshops that you can do right now:

1. Think of a person from your past or the present, from work or outside work, who comes to mind when you think someone with "presence." Got it? Usually someone pops into one's mind pretty quickly.

2. In the space below or on a piece of paper, jot down the person's name and the reasons you chose that person. List as many things as you can remember about his or her presence.

_____

_____

_____

3. Now, go back over your notes and add to them, being very specific and granular with your recollections. For instance:

   ➲   If you said the person is "confident," why do you say that? How did he enter a room, for instance, or what do you remember about his voice? How about his posture? His eye contact?

- If you said she was a good listener, what did you notice about the way she listened to other people? How could you tell she was listening?

- If you said he was a good presenter, how did he present ideas or information? Did he use a lot of facts? Did he tell stories? Did he use notes?

- Close your eyes for a moment and picture the person. What do you see? What do you recall about her facial expressions? How did she dress? Anything notable about her physical presence?

- What was this person like interpersonally? How did he act when he met you in the hallway or cafeteria? How did he act with people during meetings? How about just before or just after a meeting? Can you remember?

- Did she speak very quickly, or with a more measured pace? Did she speak loudly, or not?

- Do you recall anything particular about him when he was having a good day? How about a bad day?

- Anything else you remember that is special or unique about this person?

If you are like most people who do this exercise, you are probably surprised at how much you actually remember, even down to seemingly small details. We need to get very specific if we want to understand presence: what contributes to it, and what detracts from it.

Try doing this exercise with a number of different people from your past or present, and you'll start to notice some common themes. You will find yourself starting to make some decisions about the kind of presence you want to demonstrate.

Now, back to the activity.

4. This time, please focus on a person with presence from your work setting, past or present. In the left side of the table below, write the person's first name and list the specific behaviors and actions that you recall that demonstrate their presence.

5. Now, try to remember how it felt to be around this person. How did you *feel* as you listened to him or her deliver an important message? What was the buzz when other people found out this person was going to be part of a meeting or event? If this person was or is a leader in your business, how did other people seem to respond when they were around this leader? How did you feel when the leader noticed something special that you did? On the right side, jot down the feelings or emotions you and others experienced when this person was around.

Step 4: BEHAVIORS	Step 5: FEELINGS/REACTIONS

I ask these same questions in my workshops and record people's answers on the flip chart. On the next page are some examples of real leaders that folks in my training programs have provided. Some leaders are from their past, and some are from their current work environment. The names have been changed, of course.

BEHAVIORS	FEELINGS/REACTIONS
Conrad • Friendly and outgoing • Gives you feedback in a relaxed manner • Always well dressed, but not stuffy • Clear speaker, good tone and pace • Always has interesting things to say • Asks good questions about my work	• People enjoy working for him. • If he is on the agenda, I know it will be worthwhile. • Feel engaged • Feel like I belong, like I matter
Donna • Knows everyone's name in the department • Remembers things about your work and about you personally • Firm but fair • Great eye contact • Petite in stature but not in demeanor	• Feel like she really cares • I want to do my best for her • She disagrees sometimes, but explains it, so I feel smarter, not stupid.
Roger • We used to joke that he took "smooth" pills! Always composed under pressure. • Deep, soothing voice • Engaging, personable, friendly • Tall, maybe 6' 2" • Comfortable with everyone at every level	• He made people feel comfortable in spite of his level • I had faith in us because he had faith in us
Andie • She is often the only woman in the room because of our field, but she is so confident. • She dresses well. • She knows her stuff. • Strong voice, stands tall. Good eye contact.	• Sometimes I felt intimidated by her, but not in a bad way. I knew I had to come in with my very best stuff. • I look back now and realize how much confidence I gained by working for her.

6. Take a moment now and read what you wrote and what my workshop participants said in the columns on the right. People felt engaged, valued, included, welcomed, at ease, and *challenged*. Wow, that's impressive, right? Now imagine: What if just 25 percent of the leaders in your company were able to make people feel this way every day? What would the impact be on the health of your business?

_____

_____

_____

If you said, "higher morale, greater productivity, higher employee satisfaction, higher customer satisfaction, lower turnover, higher creativity, etc.," you are right.

And that's the bottom line—literally.

◆

These leaders had an impact on the way people felt at work. And not because they did monumentally important things or impressive things; no one was leaping tall buildings in a single bound. Instead, they focused on the little things that connected them with the people around them in subtle but impactful ways. "He remembered my wife's name." "She asked me about my kid's first day of school." "When I was in his office he never interrupted me to take a call or look at his laptop." "She said thank you."

It's the little things that leaders do every day that create the kind of environment where people feel great about being there. It's eye contact and a smile. It's attentive listening. It's "Hello" in the hallway.

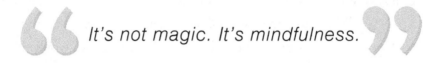

It's not magic. It's mindfulness.

Mindfulness means being very aware of what is going on right here, right now, in this interaction. It means being 100 percent present, and not distracted, disconnected, or multitasking.

I know what you're thinking: "If I don't multitask, I can't possibly get through everything I have to do in a day." That feels very true, doesn't it? However, the research would tell us that we're fooling ourselves. *Harvard Magazine* wrote about one study conducted at Stanford University in which self-described heavy multitaskers and nonmultitaskers were asked to complete certain tasks while being distracted by extraneous information.[6] The study demonstrated "habitual multitaskers felt more confident about their performance [after the test] but it was the nonmultitaskers who performed much better. Heavy multitaskers simply could not ignore the extraneous information." In other words, we fool ourselves. We think we are doing a good job of concentrating on several things at once, but in fact, we are not. This is most critical when we are multitasking while trying to pay attention to other people, such as when we are part of a conversation and simultaneously reading an e-mail or sending a text message. We think we are doing a good job, but we really aren't. Moreover, we're sending very clear signals to our conversational partner that "you just aren't that important to me right now." That's probably not our intention, but it is the perception that folks can walk away with.

The secret to being a beloved or well-respected leader is not magic. It's mindfulness. Magicians don't reveal their secrets, but this isn't magic so we will reveal all the secrets.

Mindfulness means making deliberate choices about our behavior, and then behaving. That's why the leaders who made the list on page 32 were the ones who came to mind when people thought "presence." Yes, in a corporate setting the people who are named are typically people in a position of power, but in my seminars people have also chosen a parent, a teacher, a coach, and many coworkers who were not in positions of power. "Position power" doesn't automatically imbue one with presence, which anyone in any organization will verify; nor does intellectual power. Or tall stature. Or a PhD. Presence is primarily about *being* present and the very specific cues we give off when we are or are not fully present. It's managing oneself with clarity and authenticity, and it's about being supremely *other-conscious.* More on that in Chapter Four.

Once again, I know what you are thinking. No one can do all that all the time. True. If we are being realistic, do I believe that Conrad, Donna, Roger, or Andie from page 32 never had a bad day? Of course they did. Every one of them had at least fifteen years of work experience, so the chances are pretty slim that there isn't at least one dark day or mismanaged moment in there somewhere. And yet they made the list—imperfect humans that they are— because they made really good choices most of the time consistent with their presence goals. In other words, they were *deliberate* in the way they managed themselves, their interactions, and their communication. And it worked.

And so:

> ⮌ Lots of good choices means lots of good data for others.
>
> ⮌ Consistent data create a strong pattern, which other people will support with further evidence ("halo-or-horns" effect).
>
> ⮌ Conscientious leaders make a deliberate effort to sustain the positive pattern and take action immediately to repair any damage. Thus:
>
> ⮌ People will see the repair as further evidence of the positive pattern.

Repairing Mismanaged Moments

Remember that little gadget that Tommy Lee Jones used in *Men in Black* to erase people's memories of their alien encounters? Don't you wish you could borrow that for just one day, the day after the regrettable moment occurred? Sadly, that particular gadget is not yet available, not even at Brookstone, so we have to make amends. Before we talk about how to do that, let's talk about why we should do it, not just because it's the right thing to do but because of the impact on the business.

In their book *The Cost of Bad Behavior* authors Christine Porath and Christine Pearson provide numerous examples of the specific costs a business will incur as a result of uncivil behavior. One HR manager estimated that she and the business leader spent more than ten hours dealing with an issue raised because of *one* rude e-mail sent from a corporate vice president to an employee. In straight salary alone, the HR manager estimated the cost to the company to be thousands of dollars—for one thoughtless internal email. This issue did not even involve legal counsel or incur a stress-related leave of absence, nor did her calculation include the negative impact on future productivity because of the damaged relationship.[7]

Suppose that vice president had realized what the impact of the rude e-mail would be before too much damage was done. What should he have done? Apologize immediately, of course, and make amends appropriate to the situation. Assuming he was normally a pretty reliable guy, how might the hurt employee have responded? Perhaps in a reasonable way, but certainly with a lesser degree of negativity. Consider this true example:

> *In my first month in a new company, the division president snapped at me when I caught him at a bad moment. I was devastated, and because I was new I didn't have any context or pattern to help me. When he called me in an hour later to apologize and talk to me about my project, I felt much better. Not 100 percent hip-hip-hooray-better, but much less hurt. Later, because of the fact that he'd humbled himself and apologized sincerely, and because unbecoming behavior was not part of his typical pattern, I learned to trust him and over time became one of his most loyal lieutenants.*

◆

How do effective leaders with a solid track record of "positive presence" go about repairing things after an uncharacteristically poor choice?

1. Apologize. First and foremost, once you learn that you've offended others, apologize to everyone impacted by

your behavior. You might apologize to the group if you upset your whole team, or you might apologize to people individually. Either way, do it with integrity, clarity, speed, and humanity. Keep your apology simple, but sincere. Don't overapologize.

2. Open a dialogue with the offended parties to see if there are solutions or issues that need to be addressed now that the air is clearer. Listen carefully and openly to whatever people have to say, ask questions for clarification, and don't read too much into their subtext since they still may be smarting emotionally from whatever you did earlier.

3. Don't explain why you behaved inappropriately, or at least offer only minimal explanation. Too much rationalization sounds defensive and a little desperate, and most of the time the person you offended doesn't care *why* you did it; they just care *that* you did it and you're not going to do it again.

Don't be afraid to apologize and eat a little humble pie. Leaders who can own their moments of regret and do the right thing afterward can actually strengthen people's perceptions of them. But don't push it. Remember the two charts that showed predictable and unpredictable patterns of behavior? Leader 2 had some "shining-star" moments but also lots of dark moments, and because Leader 2 is so inconsistent, people never know what to expect. There is no clear pattern there. If Leader 2 needs to repair a mismanaged moment, how likely is it people will see an apology as sincere? With that pattern, there is not much trust there to begin with.* In comparison, Leader 1 had a solid pattern of positive interaction. Look at all the stars. Now imagine

---

* Are you a "recovering" leader? See Chapter Six for a lesson on repairing the reputational damage from multiple mismanaged moments.

you could take a pencil and draw some lines connecting all those stars, you'd end up with something that looks like a strong net. This is Leader 1's virtual safety net. And guess what? It's not that difficult to repair one hole in an otherwise strong net.

> **Remember:**
>
> *Repairing the damage from a moment of regret should be done immediately, sincerely, and visibly.*

Finally, the best recovery is to avoid moments of regret in the first place. Do you know what your hot buttons are? Do you know the people or situations that trigger a powerful reaction for you? I'll bet you're thinking of a few people right now. It might seem counterintuitive to focus on the bad thing in advance, but this is an important step in managing the moment because self-awareness is the critical prelude to self-management. More on this in Chapter Three.

Let's go back to Jessica and Mark from the start of this chapter. Each was frustrated and upset and neither did a good job of managing the moment. There were unhappy consequences in both cases, and while neither person was fired or anything as dire as that, they were both deeply embarrassed.

Assuming that these dark moments are rare for each of them, what do you think they should they have done *in that exact moment* when they felt their tempers rising? Jot down your suggestions:

_____

_____

_____

Here's the process we recommend. It's easy to remember, and it works when you catch yourself in an about-to blow state:

1. Stop! Before you touch a phone or a pen or hit Send, stop and get yourself together;

2. Breathe! Take at least two long, slow, deep breaths and keep the rational part of your brain fully oxygenated. This will also slow your heart rate.

3. Think! Be mindful. Be very aware of the emotions you are feeling and manage those first, *then* start to manage the situation.

4. Act. Once you are calm, find a positive action as opposed to a negative reaction.

Unfortunately, we know that Jessica and Mark did not use this technique to ward off their regrettable moments, and so what can they learn from this experience?

_____

_____

_____

_____

If you said, "know their triggers," you are right. They were both responding to incidents that had built up over time. If they had identified and owned their triggers, each of them would have felt their bodies' early warning signals and calmed themselves before getting to a full boil.

But that did not happen either, and so each one is in repair mode. In the space below, write down what Mark and Jessica could do to begin to repair the damage.

I think Jessica should:

_____

_____

_____

_____

I think Mark should:

_____

_____

_____

_____

My suggestions are as follows:

Jessica needs to apologize for leaving a note with an offensive comment. Yes, she was well within her rights to leave a note, but her first choice should have been a note politely requesting that the SUV driver park farther away from the dividing line. That would have been a *response* to the situation, not a *reaction* to the emotion caused by the situation. Her hasty note resulted in a complaint from the SUV owner to the company's HR Department.

Because the SUV owner identified herself in the complaint, Jessica had the opportunity to apologize. The HR manager got permission to release the SUV owner's identity, and gave Jessica the option to send a note or see the SUV owner in person. To her credit, Jessica decided to apologize in person. The two women met in the atrium between their two buildings. After Jessica apologized for her choice of words, the SUV owner apologized for parking so close to Jessica's space. Her car was new and much bigger than her previous car, and she was still getting used to it. Jessica and the SUV owner may never be best friends, but the tension is greatly diminished.

Mark also needs to apologize. First, he needs to attend the next meeting of the team and apologize in person for his outburst, and his apology needs to be sincere, humble, and 100 percent excuse free. Then, he needs to open up a dialogue with the team about how he can help them regain their footing and move the project forward with more confidence. Mark should also apologize to his boss who was embarrassed by Mark's behavior. Finally, in any one-to-one meetings or phone calls he has with the people on the team, he needs to offer a personal apology for any upset he caused. If he does all of these things, and if there is enough of a pattern of positive interaction, people will see his outburst as an isolated instance and they will forgive him.

> *It is unreasonable to think that we will act perfectly in every situation. However, with greater mindfulness, we can manage more tough situations with grace and poise, and minimize the regrettable moments in our lives.*

MOMENT TO
REFLECT

❑ We don't always know what presence is,
exactly, but we know it when we see it.

❑ Moments large and small impact the way people
feel at work, which impacts their willingness
and ability to perform well at work.

❑ Leaders can choose how they want to be known,
because all it takes is mindfulness, not magic.

❑ "Up until now" can help change one's own
attachment to habitual or unproductive behaviors.

❑ There are effective, practical techniques to help us deal
with regrettable moments before and after they occur.

❑ When a solid leader makes a genuine effort to do the
right thing after a regrettable moment, people will see
the repair as further evidence of a positive pattern.

❑ Behavior change takes practice. If your career is worth
working on, your presence is worth working on.

2

LEADERS ARE NEVER INVISIBLE

Marvin has just been invited to deliver the good news of his division's recent success at an upcoming town hall meeting, the quarterly gathering where every employee is invited to listen, learn, and participate. He'll have about twenty minutes to capture their attention, acknowledge everyone's hard work, and plant the seeds to garner support for the next phase of the strategy. Marvin spends hours preparing. He vets the outline with his boss, solicits help from members of his team, gets his best designer to create the slides, and prepares a warm and witty opening anecdote that will make everyone chuckle in the first two minutes. On the day of the meeting it goes exactly as planned. It's all good.

◆

It's one data point.

Granted, it's one really big data point, but it's still only one impression, one carefully prepared and well-rehearsed performance. And everybody knows it.

You see, Marvin is not particularly warm and witty in his day-to-day interactions. Nary a chuckle escapes his lips, except in polite homage to the CEO's Monday-morning commentary about his weekend. With everyone else he is aloof. Not rude, just not engaged. No eye contact with the plebes in the hallway. No nods to folks as he carries his tray through the cafeteria, mostly because he usually eats in the executive dining room or in his office. When his ace designer walks him through the snazzy presentation slides, he acknowledges the work with a brief and impersonal "Thanks."

Hmm … lots of data points.

It's a big mistake to think that your presence only counts in those important presentations. No one I've met has an "invisibility cloak". By the time you get to the management level in most organizations, you are never "not on." It's always show time. You are always being evaluated. Every data point counts.

At this point you're probably saying to yourself, "Oh come on! That's a lot to manage when I'm already busy doing my real job." I have news for you: Being a role model, demonstrating confidence and optimism, engaging people, building relationships, and the rest of that "soft stuff" *is* your real job. It is as important to your career as your technical skills, maybe more. You know why? Because people notice—and they remember.

You know those leaders who get a standing ovation before they start their speech? *They manage all the moments.* You can, too. Through greater self-awareness (a.k.a. mindfulness) you *can* create the impression you want to create and, more importantly, be the best person you can be at work: fully engaged and engaging, totally in the moment, and having a positive impact on the people around you. You will be the leader people think of when they think of "presence."

Presence Is a "Pre-sense"

Years ago when my friend Bill Young and I were collaborating on a new presentation skills and presence seminar, we were trying to define "presence" in a memorable way. I was trying to make a connection to the word "prescience" meaning having foreknowledge of something, but Bill came up with something even better. "Presence is a 'pre-sense.' It's easy to understand and remember because it's embedded in the word," he declared, and so it is.

But a pre-sense of what?

What Should One Know in Advance in Order to Have Strong Presence?

In our view, people successfully manage their presence when they have a clear pre-sense of:

> 1. How they come across
>
> 2. What others expect of them

It makes sense. If I have a clear pre-sense of how I come across, and if I know what they are expecting of me in a given situation, I can successfully deliver the goods. I can speak well, listen well, stay present, and manage all the moments.

- How I come across has a lot to do with both my message content and my body language. Often, people are unaware of something they are communicating through their body language. We call this *subtext*, and we'll talk more about it later in this chapter.

- What others expect of me will shift depending on the *context*. We'll talk more about this in Chapter Four.

- Managing the moment means actively working to understand both—namely, I know how I come across and can manage text and subtext to ensure my effectiveness, *and* I know what this audience expects of me in this situation and am prepared to deliver.

Our Presence Model

It's easier to understand seemingly intangible things when we have a model that pulls it all together. Our presence model looks at the behavioral and emotional elements of presence in three categories as well as in the areas of overlap. The next four chapters dig more deeply into those elements. Consider the model holistically first:

I.   Self-Awareness and Self-Management

You can't manage what you don't know. It's hard to "manage the moment" if you don't know what data points you are putting out there. You need an objective sense of how you come across, on good days and bad, so that you know which strengths to sustain and which potential liabilities to overcome. Self-awareness is a critical component of presence. Chapter Three contains more examples, tools, and exercises.

II.   Interpersonal Skills

Presence is only presence if you are with someone. There are dozens of fine books devoted entirely to interpersonal effectiveness if you want more study, but our emphasis will be on those specific elements that help you be more *other-conscious* and *connect* to others in more meaningful and authentic ways. Chapter Four is devoted to this topic.

III.   Communication and Brand

Of all the tasks large and small that leaders and managers perform, very little gets done without some sort of communication. *Communication is your presence in action.* Whether it is in a meeting, on a conference call, or in a text message, every time you communicate, it is a demonstration of your presence. You'll find tools, activities, and more case studies in Chapter Five. *Your brand is how you want to be known.* It is part of the right circle because every time you communicate, you have the opportunity to further your brand. Chapter Six will focus on some of the practical aspects of creating and strengthening your brand, as well as how brand can directly impact your presence and vice versa.

Together, the three circles of presence ensure that when you show up, it is the very best you. Every time.

Simple, but Not Easy.

The model is simple. The skills are not easy. Anthropologists, linguists, behaviorists, and even the folks who sell used cars all study human interaction in great detail in order to (a) understand it, and (b) manage it to a certain outcome. We're all just trying to understand one another, and yet our verbal and nonverbal communication is loaded with opportunities for misinterpretation.

For instance, consider this seemingly benign conversation at my house not long ago:

"We're having chicken for supper again tonight, okay?"

"Fine."

Can you tell just by looking at these words if this was a positive or negative interaction? Well, you can if you've had the same conversation at your house. In that case, you have your data to fill in any gaps because you were there. You heard and saw the conversation, and you have your own context to supply the emotions. But you don't know the context at my house, and you are missing some valuable communication clues because all you have are the printed words. So, here's a little more data:

Suppose I told you that the night before this exchange we had our very favorite chicken dish and there was just enough left for this evening's supper? And suppose we put an exclamation point after the word "Fine!" Now what do you think about our brief exchange? Right. Happy people, no problem.

Let's change it up a bit: Suppose I told you that we already had chicken three times in the past five days and one of us was getting pretty tired of it. Imagine the face and voice of that response, "Fine." Suppose it was also preceded by a heavy sigh exhaled through the teeth. Now how would you characterize the interaction? Right. Not so fine.

Without knowing more about how those lines were delivered and the history and emotions underlying that delivery, you can't fully grasp the meaning just from the words on the page.

"And Just What Do You Mean by That?"

One of the things that makes adult interaction so challenging is we have to manage both text and subtext:

⊃ The *text* refers to the actual words being spoken or written. We will also refer to it as content.

⊃ *Subtext* is the subjective meaning conveyed by the delivery of those words and influenced by the context and circumstances. When we are interacting with people in person or on the phone, subtext is conveyed by visible body language and vocal variations, which we will refer to respectively as elements of look and sound. More specifics on these elements will be covered in Chapter Five.

➲ Subtext is created mechanically, but informed emotionally. By "mechanically," I mean the physical manifestation that people see or hear, such as a squint or a "tsk" sound. However, there is an underlying reason for that squint or sound that is related to how a person feels about the item in question. For instance, if I am genuinely happy that there is a little more of that tasty chicken for dinner, I will smile, make eye contact, and respond with a bright lift in my voice, "Fine!" If I am unhappy with the menu but feel I have no choice, I might pull down one corner of my mouth, roll my eyes, sigh audibly, and speak in a flat tone, "Fine." The mechanics are informed by the emotion.

We encounter subtext all the time. Consider this poor fellow:

"She's texting me, but I think she's also subtexting me."

The New Yorker, July 2, 2007. Used by permission.

Our Romeo is trying to figure out what she really means in her text message. We've all been there; we're constantly trying to interpret both the text and the subtext of any interaction, and we never feel we have enough data. That's why people use those little symbols known as *emoticons* in their e-mails or text messages. It's the shorthand way to add some subtext to the bare words of the text so that our meaning is not misconstrued. For example, suppose I sent you one of the three text-message replies below. How would you interpret each reply? In other words, what's the subtext?

Your text message to me: "Did U hear? Kevin is off the project."

How would you interpret each example of my text message back to you?

1. Too bad _____

2. Too bad ☹ _____

3. Too bad ☺ _____

The first one is impossible to know without the context, meaning the recipient (you) can interpret it any way you want. The second one suggests I will miss Kevin. The third one is a little snarky; the juxtaposition of the "sad" words with the happy face could almost be interpreted as sarcasm. Now if you respond to number three with an "LOL," that will tell me that you're pretty glad to see Kevin gone as well.

Take another look at the cartoon on page 52. Our hapless Romeo may only have his Juliet's words, or perhaps she dropped in an emoticon, but we will never know. Romeo knows because he also has some context from his relationship. Maybe that's why he looks a little panic stricken. But we don't know. We can only guess based on the data that we have.

In most situations, our successful interpretation depends on the degree to which data from look, sound and content are available, and the degree to which they are aligned. When our words are supported by the expected facial expressions, gestures, vocal melody, and volume, appropriate for the situation and audience, the meaning is clearer and the message resounds. Leaders who successfully integrate text and subtext are able to engage and motivate others more readily than leaders who send confusing or conflicting signals.

Mixed Messages

Mixed messages are those communiqués where the text and subtext are at odds. Perhaps the most important and influential research on the impact of mixed messages was done by UCLA psychology professor Albert Mehrabian and published in his 1971 book *Silent Messages*. Mehrabian was curious about how people resolve the inconsistency when look, sound, and content are not aligned. His research showed that when messages were mixed, the impact of the delivery was as follows:

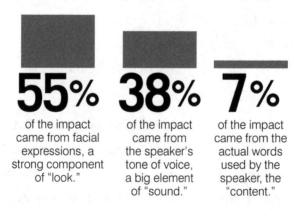

55% of the impact came from facial expressions, a strong component of "look."

38% of the impact came from the speaker's tone of voice, a big element of "sound."

7% of the impact came from the actual words used by the speaker, the "content."

There are dozens of books, articles, and training programs that focus on body language, but Mehrabian[8] was one of the first people to prove that when the total message is mixed, the audience pays the *least* amount of attention to the actual words. At the time of its publication, this was big news to business people who assumed that a presentation of the facts, delivered in a clear and logical manner, was all that they needed.

Well, it wasn't enough then, and it's not enough now.

What is missing in most business presentations, then and now, is emotion. Without emotion, there is no meaning, no subtext, no passion. Without emotion, there is no engagement. But just like my "duh" moment in the introduction, we fail to make that obvious connection. And why?

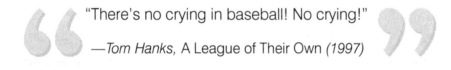

"There's no crying in baseball! No crying!"
—*Tom Hanks,* A League of Their Own *(1997)*

In other words, we strive for stoicism under the mistaken belief that emotions don't belong at work. This, of course, is a myth. If you try to squeeze all of the emotion out of a presentation or conversation in a (misguided) effort to appear more business-like, all you are doing is appearing cold, impersonal, and inauthentic. Still, there are folks who are uncomfortable with emotional expression at work, even positive emotions, and especially the ones that are scary, such as crying.[9] I actually had a boss tell me that I was "too happy" at work. Really? So I should cheer *down*? I can laugh at it now, but at the time I felt real pressure to dial back the smiling to something more neutral, which in turn made me feel less happy. So I guess *that* worked, but I also felt inauthentic and constrained.

> *We think we do a good job of masking our emotions by faking our body language, but often the only person fooled is us.*

Remember, subtext is created mechanically but informed emotionally. Most people try to manage subtext by performing the mechanics separately from the emotion. This is what we refer to as managing subtext from the outside in like people trying to cheer up by putting on a fake smile when they aren't very happy. They may also add an unnaturally bright and brittle tone of voice to seem as if they are in a bright and cheery mood when they really aren't. However, others can usually spot the disconnect (especially if they are looking for it) and will begin to wonder about the subtext. They don't know on a conscious level that they are spotting a mixed message, but they sense that something isn't quite right. Remember what we said about patterns in Chapter One? Well, people will look for other clues to make sense of the mixed message, and they will connect the dots in a way that makes sense to them. Once it makes sense, it *becomes* true—to them.

Note that the outside-in approach actually does work for formal presentations when the speaker creates the message content, polishes it, and then deliberately practices managing the mechanics—namely, changes in gesture, voice, facial expression, and so forth—in order to ensure alignment. This works especially well when the communicator has a clear point of view about the message and works to highlight that point of view with aligned look and sound elements.

 "I am a human being. Nothing human is alien to me."
—*Terence (163 BC)*

A better way to manage subtext is from the inside out, which means we get really clear on our emotions first. Then, we manage the degree to which we express those emotions and what is appropriate for the situation and audience. When we are clear on our own feelings and relatively unobstructed in the expression of our content, we can be fully authentic. However, in many business settings today leaders get stuck when they have to hide their feelings, because they are asked to deliver a message that they don't believe in or agree with. The default is that the communicators usually deliver the message with a degree of (fake) enthusiasm or, worse, with no emotional affect at all. This is ineffective, inauthentic, stressful[10]—and very common.

Hmm ... So How Am I Doing at Managing My Subtext?

Good question! Here's a little quiz:

How often do you...	Daily, Weekly, Occasionally, Never
1. hear yourself saying, "But that's not what I meant!"	
2. notice people frowning after you say something that you thought was positive?	
3. use sarcastic humor and notice people aren't laughing or responding in kind?	
4. hear people say to you, "there's no reason to get upset over this" or even "please lower your voice" and you didn't realize you were upset?	
5. have your direct reports tell you, "I didn't realize this was so important to you"?	
6. make an effort to keep your feelings to yourself?	
7. skip the step of checking in with your emotions before communicating something important?	

If you were able to write "never" in all seven boxes on the right side of the grid, you are doing a great job of managing subtext. People are receiving your messages in the way that you intend. If the frequency is "occasionally" or more, you need to pay more attention to how you are expressing yourself. Notice that the first five questions have to do with how other people respond to you. Their response is always a big clue as to the effectiveness of your delivery. The last two questions are more internal about how you manage your emotions.

Now I know what some of you are thinking: "Jeepers, do we have to talk about feelings all the time?"

Yes, we do, because if talking about feelings frustrates you, dear reader, there is very little hope that you will successfully align your text and subtext and communicate in ways that inspire and motivate others. Very simply, there will be no magic.

We see it all the time. Sometimes when I'm helping someone prepare for a presentation, and I see they are expressing little or no emotion, I ask them how they feel about their subject, and they reply, "I don't know." You would be amazed at how many times people don't stop to acknowledge or even think about their feelings. Usually they are too busy focusing on the nuts and bolts of the content. Other times it simply never occurs to them. But many simply deny their own feelings and carry on with their assignment like Spock on a mission. I understand this. I worked in corporate America for more than twenty years. The fact is we tamp down our emotions so much at work that we're not sure *how* we feel at times. Sometimes we ignore our emotions in the mistaken belief we can work our way logically and efficiently through the day; other times we bury our emotions because we don't have a safe way to deal with them at the office.

Whatever the reason, if you are a leader and you are seeking to engage others, a better choice is to first *acknowledge* your emotions and then find a way to communicate authentically. This is the inside-out approach to aligning text and subtext and we'll spend a lot more time on this in Chapter Five. Until then, consider the story of Sondra:

> *Sondra was a vice president in a large financial services company. Well respected and well liked, she was the natural choice to replace her boss who left the division for another opportunity overseas. Now she was a part of the EC, the Executive Committee. In order to fit in, Sondra watched the other EC members carefully and modified her naturally expressive style to be more contained, which was appropriate for her new role and level. Six months into the new role, Sondra made a well-informed but bold decision that unfortunately did not fully pan out and caused a great deal of backtracking and rework in her department.*
>
> *Sondra is not one to dwell on her mistakes or other people's mistakes for that matter. Her natural response was always to roll up her sleeves and say, "Okay, how do we fix this now, and how do we ensure it doesn't happen again?" Sondra had to admit that for a number of very good reasons she made a bad decision, and so at a large, all-hands meeting, Sondra took responsibility for the decision, and in her familiar open and expressive manner, apologized to the staff for causing them additional work. She offered her support to anyone who needed it, answered a few questions from the audience, and ended the meeting. Immediately afterward, one of the other EC members came up to her and said, "A word to the wise: never apologize like that. It was not a good move on your part. Now they will question everything you do." Sondra was*

stunned. Her gut told her to speak from the heart, own the problem, and move to fix it. But she was still new to the EC. Maybe she should have played it more neutrally or used the reasons and rationale as a smokescreen. "Oh boy," she thought as she walked slowly back to her office. "Was this another 'dumb' decision? Maybe I'm just too emotional. Maybe I should have just disappeared into the woodwork for awhile."

Let's pause for a moment in the story of Sondra. What do you think of Sondra's choice to apologize publicly?

_____

_____

_____

Let's see what her people thought:

Sondra continued to ponder as she took the five-minute walk back to her office. However, by the time she reached her desk, her phone and IM were ringing and pinging like crazy. Other managers, employees, and even her boss were praising her speech. One employee wrote to her, "Now I know what leadership is supposed to look like!" Her boss said, "I thought you had guts when I put you in this job, and now I know I was right."

◆

Sondra learned a really valuable lesson: Her apology worked for her, not against her, because she was authentic, honest, and sincere. She remained visible, not invisible, and she took responsibility for the decision and was willing to be vulnerable and own it publically. People saw that and they appreciated it. In their eyes, her apology simply reinforced the already strong pattern of her presence.

PREMISE #5

Leadership Is both More Personal and More Public Than Ever Before

For those readers who have been working for twenty years or more, think about the changes you've seen: Twenty-plus years ago there were no "town hall" meetings in corporations, and very few opportunities to mingle outside one's level. That's all changed now.

- ➲ Your leadership is more public because today's organizations are flatter, with fewer layers of management and broader spans of control. Most organizations operate in a fluid, highly matrixed format where employees routinely work with people above their level, below their level, across division or department lines, and so forth. So leaders are more visible internally than ever before.

- ➲ As business leaders become media stars, we see our leaders spotlighted on cable news shows, on the front cover of business journals, or in the financial section of the newspaper. This was quite rare years ago, but with so many business news outlets, they need to expand coverage in order to fill the time or space. So they go beyond the CEOs of giant companies and interview or write about more and more "local" business executives.

➲ It's also more public because of e-mails, IMs, social media, and cell phone cameras. Think about it: Have you ever gotten an e-mail chain and scrolled all the way down to the bottom and found something you probably weren't supposed to see? It is very easy for any e-document to be circulated quickly, both internally and externally. Juicy or unfortunate e-mails get forwarded internally like wildfire or, even worse, end up in the press or one of the business blogs before you can blink.

➲ It's more personal because people today are rightfully skeptical about their leaders and they want to know: Who is this leader and what does he believe in? Is this someone I want to follow? Let's face it, we have all seen way too many disgraced leaders in big business, not to mention in our communities, our churches, and our country. The younger generations in the workforce reflect some of the same idealism the Baby Boomers felt in the 1960s. The "millennials" are now the ones buying ecofriendly consumables and hybrid cars. They want something or someone to believe in, and they will believe in their leaders *if* those leaders win their trust and engage their passions.

In other words, workers today are looking for ways to connect—to the mission, the vision, and their leaders. When you can remove the clutter around your presence and be known to them, you create the opportunity for both passion and focus. Visible, not invisible.

Keep Spinning Those Plates!

Yes, you are busy. You have meetings to attend, budgets to prepare, reviews to deliver, and customers to serve ... and now we're asking you to manage emotions and be mindful of your subtext ... really? You're probably thinking you can barely keep the plates spinning as

it is. Let me explain this metaphor for our younger readers. Those of you over a certain age (or if you've seen reruns of the old Ed Sullivan Show) will recall the act where a man would spin china plates on flexible sticks attached to the floor.

The audience grew evermore impressed and nervous as he put more and more plates in motion at the same time. Once in a while one of the plates would start to wobble and the audience would gasp until the man dashed to the tipping plate and revved it up again, averting disaster.

Managing your presence while you're doing your "real job" is a lot like keeping the plates spinning. Not only must you pay attention to both the content and delivery of your messages in an audience-centric way, but you must also understand and manage your own emotions (wobble, wobble), read other people's body language (wobble, wobble), listen thoroughly and openly, and be situationally and contextually aware. Whew!

But that's not all.

You may be familiar with the 1950 Japanese movie *Rashomon*, the theme of which has been repeated in everything from sitcoms to bestseller novels. The movie shows the same tragic event through the eyes of four different witnesses, each of whom has his own very distinctive point of view. The movie is considered a cinematic classic. Watching it, the audience can't help but be both amazed and dismayed by the fact that all four points of view are "correct." The dismay comes from our collective realization that we have done this very same thing—argued over the details of an event—because our perspective colors our memory. In fact, the term "Rashomon effect" has come to describe the effect of the subjectivity of an observer on his or her memory of an event.

The Rashomon effect is alive and well in today's organizations. Take a look at this example of a conversation between four coworkers leaving a meeting:

"So does Jerry want to see the draft or the final document by Friday?"

"I'm not sure. I think he wants the draft."

"I thought he wanted us to give the draft to Jane by Friday so she could look at it first."

"That's not what I heard."

Which one of these interpretations is correct? At the moment, they all are. And having been one of the four people engaged in this very real conversation, this discussion went on for another ten minutes. What a waste of time and energy. And who is responsible for this confusion? Jerry is responsible, and it happened all the time. Invariably, one of us would troop back to his office and ask for clarification, which took another ten minutes. Here's the thing: Jerry had no idea he was causing this problem until we finally brought it to his attention. I'll bet you've encountered your own "Jerry" once or twice in your career, haven't you? Remember how it felt to work for him or her?

If you are the leader, you have to own the fact that your best and most loyal people are going to try to do what you ask them to do, to the extent that they understand what you want. If they are confused or go down the wrong path, it's because *you* weren't clear. And many leaders know this, but they tell me it's because they "don't have time" to communicate carefully. Really? Remember Alan Fine's comment about knowing what to do but not always doing what we know? Shortchanging your communication is a mistake. There's a lot at stake here, not the least of which is your coworkers' productivity and your reputation. Careful communication doesn't take that much longer. When I coach folks preparing for any sort of presentation, we can get clear on their purpose and the right approach in about five minutes.

> *For every interaction related to something important, be clear on your purpose and plan your approach in advance.*

Let's go back to the story of Marvin from the beginning of this chapter.

Q: Over 150 people were in the audience during Marvin's town hall speech that day. They all saw and heard the exact same words at the exact same time. How many different interpretations of that speech do you think there are?

Answer: Somewhere between 1 and 150, but it is likely on the low side because of his careful preparation.

Q: Now, how many different interpretations are there for his hallway or cafeteria-line behavior?

Answer: Who knows? Certainly not Marvin, because it hasn't occurred to him to have a purpose for his cafeteria interactions. However, he has accomplished something and it ain't good, and I'll bet Marvin would be shocked that people feel marginalized or disrespected by him because of his coldness and lack of engagement.

Marvin didn't intend to insult people, but that was the impact of his actions, from his lack of eye contact to the absence of sincere thanks. In their book *The Cost of Bad Behavior* authors Christine Pearson and Christine Porath define incivility as "the exchange of seemingly inconsequential inconsiderate words and deeds that violate conventional norms of workplace conduct." They go on to say, "Incivility as we define it is not an objective phenomenon; it reflects people's subjective *interpretation* of actions and how these actions make them feel."[11] And guess what? Oftentimes there is a big disconnect between what the offender and the offendee deem to be hurtful. Recently, I was teaching a seminar where the participants make presentations on the last day. There is a fair amount of pressure since the participants are evaluated by a panel of judges. One of the more introverted participants had been speaking for about two minutes when the door opened noisily and one of the younger participants strolled in, an hour late, holding her coffee. She proceeded to stroll in front of him and then walk around looking for a seat in the front of the room, seemingly oblivious to the fact that she was distracting both the speaker and the audience. The presenter lost his place for a moment, then recovered pretty well and finished strong. Afterward, he told me how distracted he was by the latecomer and how upsetting it was to him that she could be so thoughtless and rude to a colleague. Meanwhile the latecomer made no apologies. She didn't think she had done anything "wrong" since she was late for a valid reason. There's that disconnect.

ACTIVITY

Look back at Jessica and Mark from the beginning of Chapter One. Which one of them was uncivil?

_____

_____

_____

_____

Answer: You probably answered that Mark was uncivil, but the truth is they both were. Yes, Mark ripped the phone out of the wall, very dramatic, while Jessica simply wrote a tactless note in reply to what she saw as her parking garage neighbor's thoughtless behavior. Pearson and Porath say, "Incivility doesn't have to involve a lot of drama. It can occur when workers are simply disrespectful, inconsiderate, tactless, insensitive, uncaring or rude to one another."[12] We might feel sympathy for Jessica and agree that her note was just a flippant bit of nothing, no malice intended. But that's *her* interpretation of her note, not the SUV owner's interpretation. The SUV owner was offended, and Jessica had a bigger mess to clean up.

◆

A C T I V I T Y

Imagine you are Marvin's coach. Based on the brief description of the presence model, what do you think Marvin should focus on the most in order to strengthen his presence?

_____

_____

_____

_____

Marvin appears to have strong presentations skills and he knows how to prepare. Great! He has a strong base upon which he can build. And he will need that strong base because he is clearly in a position of some power and influence, but without greater self-awareness and stronger interpersonal skills, he's missing opportunities to fully engage others when he's not on stage. Marvin's coach might encourage him to:

⮑ Invite one or more colleagues join him for lunch in the cafeteria so he can be seen doing more social and less exclusive activities. Eventually branch out to join other groups for lunch.

- ➲ Make eye contact and say hello to people in the hallway, elevators, and parking garage. Eventually expand that to remember and use people's names.

- ➲ Pay attention to the things people do to please him and compliment those people generously, including details that demonstrate that he really noticed the effort or outcome. Eventually expand that to praise other people to their bosses.

- ➲ Devote a few minutes at the start and end of mixed-level meetings to engage in a little small talk so people can get to know him better, and vice versa. Eventually expand that to remember personal details about folks (kids, hobbies, sports teams, etc.) so he can ask about them.

- ➲ Remember that every interaction he has with others is a chance to demonstrate his presence. Begin by deciding how he wants to be known, and connect that to specific behaviors.

◆

Marvin and I worked together before the big push to virtual in 2020, and I can only imagine how difficult it would be for Marvin to create connections with people via videoconferencing. All of the suggestions above still apply, and in addition, Marvin will need to keep his camera on and make sure people see he is 100 percent focused on *this* conversation.

MOMENT TO
REFLECT

- ❑ Leaders are never invisible, and thus must manage all the moments.

- ❑ Having a pre-sense of how you come across and what others expect is critical to managing your presence.

- ❑ Mixed messages confuse and confound others. Leaders who do a good job with managing subtext are better able to engage others.

- ❑ Emotions do belong at work and when properly managed can be used to connect, inspire and motivate others.

- ❑ Incivility is in the eye of the beholder. Effective leaders take time to communicate thoughtfully and thoroughly.

3

KNOW THYSELF

Sara was a rising star. Hard-working and personable, she brought 100 percent to every endeavor. The last project she was assigned to came in on time and satisfied all requirements. Colleagues enjoyed working with her, and her boss was pleased with the way Sara responded to each new challenge. However, when he recommended her promotion, Sara's boss was told that in spite of her accomplishments, Sara was seen as "too young and immature." Sara's boss pressed for details. "Well, have you ever noticed her in meetings? She twirls her hair like a ten-year-old. No, she's not ready."

◆

Ron is in charge of strategic planning for the largest division of a well-known company in the USA. A former consultant working now for the company, Ron was brought in to help other leaders create more comprehensive forecasts for their business. Ron was well suited for this role. Intelligent and well educated, he brought a quick mind and big-picture viewpoint that helped his colleagues think beyond their silos and stay "out of the weeds." Unfortunately, people generally avoided having these useful conversations with Ron because Ron is a talker. And he talks and he talks and he talks, and once those ideas start flowing, Ron's quick mind creates more and more connections and his excitement causes every meeting and conversation to run long. Really long.

◆

Sara and Ron have one important thing in common: They both have annoying and potentially career-limiting habits, and neither of them is aware of it. And if you don't know about it, you can't fix it.

Now, we can argue the fairness or unfairness of stalling someone's career because of hair twirling another time because the fact is it is true. Sara twirls her hair. She also tilts her head slightly to the side when she is presenting at meetings, and she looks younger than her actual age. These three data points taken together are translating as "little girl" in the senior boss's mind.

Fair? Probably not.

Fixable? Definitely, especially if Sara is made aware of the behaviors and their potential impact, because what you don't know can hurt you.

But wait. Before you think disparaging thoughts about the big boss for giving so much weight to hair twirling, let's consider his point of view. Right now the big boss doesn't know if he can rely on Sara's maturity under pressure. If promoted she would be expected to make presentations to more senior people, and the big boss is not willing to compromise his reputation. There is a risk that other senior folks would question his judgment if she is not ready. Knowing this is the underlying concern, Sara and her manager can help her create new habits that will ensure the big boss sees and hears more data points that show her readiness and fewer that distract from her knowledge and experience.

Let's revisit Ron for a moment. Unlike Sara he is already in a senior position, and so the impact of his lack of awareness is actually greater. When Ron overtalks at a meeting, there is a ripple effect. Most obviously there is the loss of time and money resulting from wasted meeting time. The other people in Ron's meetings are usually high-level professionals being paid high salaries, so every hour wasted can be translated to real dollars. There is also the intangible loss arising from potentially productive conversations in or outside meetings that never happen because people know there is no such thing as a short conversation with Ron, and they simply don't have the time. "Great guy," they say, "But too verbose."

Is *this* fixable? We shall see later in this chapter.

Self-Management Can Only Come With Self-Awareness

You saw the three circles of our presence model in Chapter Two. In this chapter we are going to drill down into the components of the top circle: self-awareness and self-management.

But first, let's define "self-awareness" and make sure we are clear on the difference between self-awareness and self-consciousness, because:

we want you to be supremely self-aware, but not at all self-conscious.

How are they different? In the space below, define each and describe the difference in your own words:

_____

_____

_____

_____

How does your answer compare with the following explanation?

- ➲ Self-awareness is knowledge and acceptance of one's strengths and weaknesses in as objective a manner as possible; this knowledge has come through reliable and specific feedback that is taken seriously.

- ➲ Self-consciousness is a form of awareness, but it is usually poorly informed and thus is more subjective and unreliable. It *is* an aspect of our behavior or personality that we think other people will have an opinion about. Self-consciousness often has a judgment attached, and that judgment is not usually kind or generous. It often shows up as a little voice in our head criticizing something that we're doing.

Here's the thing: If I am being self-conscious about something, I am "in my head" listening to or arguing with the little voice, and therefore I am not "in the room," fully present and participating. Instead, I am preoccupied, inhibited, and possibly inauthentic because of that little voice.

How do you silence that nagging little voice? By recognizing the subjectivity of self-consciousness (it's not real; it's *your idea of what's real*) and focusing your energy on what matters.

PREMISE #6

Objective Self-awareness Is a Precondition to Being Present

If you agree with this premise, how do we get the little voice to back off so we can be more fully in the moment? Try this technique:

> Step 1: Listen to what the voice is saying. What is it all agitated about? And is it right? Partially right? If so, then in an offstage moment address whatever it is that the voice is trying to tell you. If the voice is not correct, skip directly to Step 3.

> Step 2: When you've done all you can to get rid of issue behind that nagging self-doubt, give yourself a positive affirmation just before presenting that is the opposite of what the voice is saying, as shown in the table below.

> Step 3: Finally, when you're presenting or participating in the meeting and the little voice pops into your head, tell it "I'm busy! I'll listen to you later," and refocus.

The Nagging Voice	Our Response
"I never should have worn this outfit on such an important day! It doesn't even fit right. I need to lose ten pounds ..."	You aren't going to lose ten pounds by Tuesday's meeting. Purchase and/or tailor a special outfit that makes you feel great and wear it on important days. Then tell yourself, "I look and feel really terrific today!"
"I can hear myself rambling on and on. Why didn't I prepare and practice more instead of answering stupid e-mails until midnight? Now they're going to think I don't know my stuff."	Make a firm resolution to put yourself first and give yourself plenty of time to prepare your key messages. Edit them for clarity and brevity, and practice the tough ones out loud. Then tell yourself, "I know my stuff and I'm ready to share it."
"Oh no, they asked me a question. Everyone is looking at me. My face is turning red. I can feel it. Why does this always happen?"	Anticipate questions and prepare and practice answers before going to meetings. Practice calming techniques before and during the meeting. Then tell yourself, "I am ready. Bring it!"
Your turn! My nagging voice says,	To address the issue, I will do the following: Then I will tell myself:

Do any of those worries in the left column sound familiar? Now read the right column straight down and tell me: What impact would those actions and positive affirmations have on someone's presence?

_____

_____

_____

Yes, the impact would be a very positive one. The behaviors on the right demonstrate confidence, control, and poise—good leadership qualities. That's why it is important to pay attention to the things that undermine one's confidence; those little insecurities show up as subtext that people might misinterpret. When you listen to the little voice (outside the high-pressure event), you learn more about yourself so you have the information you need to improve whatever it is that needs improving. You empower yourself. You can now make new choices that influence how others will see you.

Heads Up's Presence Model: Self-Awareness and Self-Management

SELF-AWARENESS & SELF-MANAGEMENT

Knows one's strengths and weaknesses; demonstrates optimism, flexibility, courage, resilience; listens patiently; manages emotional triggers.

Self-Awareness and Self-Management:

- ➲ Knows one's strengths and weaknesses

- ➲ Demonstrates optimism, flexibility, courage, resilience

- ➲ Listens patiently

- ➲ Manages emotional triggers

Objective Knowledge of One's Strengths and Weaknesses

You know that great feeling when you are playing a sport or a musical instrument, or engaging in any activity that you love and you're at the top of your game? When we master a particular skill, there's a feeling of freedom that, in turn, allows us to push further and further beyond our earlier limitations. "Mastery" literally means we are the master. So why are some people uncomfortable talking about their strengths? Sure, it might be due to a lack of consistent feedback that helps them calibrate their own understanding of their skills. Or it might be due to a sense of modesty that prevails in some countries or gender cultures. They don't want to sound as if they are bragging. However, in most Western business environments, we need to be able to talk objectively about our skills and strengths. Consider the fact that many performance reviews today require the individual to write a self-assessment. The ability to gracefully and objectively acknowledge one's strengths, achievements, and skills is essential in order to accurately represent oneself.

For some people, it's easier to talk about a weakness than a strength. In fact, some folks can and will recite a list of all their flaws at the drop of a hat. It's an interesting but misguided choice. The speaker might intend to show their humility or even their hard-headed realism. However, reciting such a list can be perceived as "begging for a compliment" from the listener who then feels forced to disagree, for surely no one who works here (or who is in this family, or who is my friend) can have that many flaws! Don't go there. Be objective about your strengths and your weaknesses.

Assuming that people really want to get better at their jobs, stretch themselves, develop, grow, and succeed, they need to know exactly *where* to focus their developmental energies. Knowing what to work on is quite freeing and exciting to achievement-focused individuals. I used to have a young analyst working for me who would come into my office to get guidance when she got stuck. We would sit and brainstorm a bit, and when she finally saw the solution clearly she would literally jump out of my guest chair with a big smile on her face and rush back to her desk, eager to apply the solution. I don't think her feet touched the floor. She was energized and empowered by knowing exactly how to solve her problem.

Knowledge is power. Without knowledge of both strengths and weaknesses, you don't know what tools you have in your personal toolkit that you can rely on in good times and in bad, and you don't know which potential liabilities need managing before too many unwanted data points get out there.

We've already seen what happened with Sara and Ron because they lacked knowledge of a potential weakness.

Do you know? And can you be objective about your strengths and weaknesses? Let's see.

ACTIVITY

What skills and strengths do you bring to your current job? Are any of these unique to you? Do they set you apart? Where could you be stronger? What are your relative weaknesses, and can you minimize their impact by emphasizing certain strengths or partnering with a colleague whose gifts differ from yours?

_____

_____

_____

_____

Now, can you validate your list so that you can be objective? What feedback have you received from your boss or from comments in a 360° feedback report? Do you have a trusted colleague who can help you reality-test the list? What do they see as strengths you should leverage and weaknesses to work on?

_____

_____

_____

As you look at your strengths and weaknesses, which ones do you want to pay attention to, how might you do that, and what is the upside to focusing on those items? How will this effort benefit your presence? How will it highlight your unique qualities?

_____

_____

_____

Remember, knowledge is power, even if that knowledge is a little hard to take at first. When people walk into one of my presence seminars for the first time, they usually notice the video camera set up in the back of the room. Often one or two people will groan out loud and at least one person will say "I hate watching myself on video!" Let's face it: Very few people actually look forward to the video experience. After explaining to them that we will only watch the recordings during the private coaching sessions and not as a group, they tend to calm down. Then I ask them: "If you had an unconscious habit that was impacting the way people perceive you at work, would you rather know about it, or continue to not know?"

Yep, they'd rather know, and so would you. Objective knowledge of your strengths and weaknesses gives you the power. That's why we say: Solid, helpful feedback is "the gift that keeps on giving."

◆

Let's finish looking at the first circle of the presence model on page 77. Let me ask you: If someone can demonstrate the following four emotional intelligence qualities as behaviors, what would be the impact on that person's presence and leadership? Think about it and make some notes below.

➲ Optimism

➲ Flexibility

➲ Courage

➲ Resilience

_____

_____

_____

_____

_____

These four qualities are essential to strong presence:

➲ Optimism. Someone needs to demonstrate the powerful, positive belief that we can achieve the goal or overcome the obstacles before us. The optimistic leader is one who can infuse a challenging situation with the confidence we need to soldier on. Optimism doesn't mean pie-eyed self-delusion. Instead, it is realism tinged with hope, as well as confidence in oneself and in others.

➲ Flexibility. The flexible leader is one who can read a situation and flex his style or actions to achieve a better outcome. This demands that the leader be fully present and in the moment, open to text and subtext, to emotion as well as to logic, so that both the leader and followers can envision workable solutions.

➲ Courage. By definition, leaders are out in front. The courageous leader is one who can manage her own emotions, doubts, or fears in order to keep herself and her followers moving forward into unknown and untried territories. The courageous leader is one who is not afraid to speak up or offer a point of view when needed.

➲ Resilience. No one is perfect. We all make mistakes. The resilient leader is one who bounces back from disappointment, embarrassment, or failure with courage and optimism. Resilient leaders demonstrate to others that it is okay to try new things and take intelligent risks because mistakes don't cripple them. Instead, mistakes are learning experiences that inform future thinking and foster creativity and courage in others (as with Sondra in Chapter Two).

Emotional intelligence qualities appear in many of the stories, case studies, and tools in this book. The fact is that leaders who truly "show up" demonstrate all of the above. They are aware of their own emotions and manage them appropriately in order to connect, motivate, reassure, or even inspire others. Take a look at the descriptions again and ask yourself, "How does this behavior show up for me? When do I demonstrate optimism, flexibility, courage, and resilience? What habitual behaviors of mine might keep people from experiencing me in this way?"

Listening and Presence

There are some who say that listening is an art while others say it is a science. In our model, it is a behavior. In fact, listening is so critical to presence that it reappears in different forms throughout the model. In the top circle of the model, the listening skill we are looking at is "Listens patiently."

What is "patient listening" and what does it have to do with self-awareness and self-management?

_____

_____

_____

_____

Patient listening is disciplined, focused listening where we wait until the other person is finished before formulating a response and starting our reply. Patient listening is hard. It takes incredible self-awareness (to know what makes us impatient) and self-management (to control the impulse to think ahead or jump in).

When do we listen impatiently?

- When we already know what they are going to say, so we say it for them;

- When it takes the other person too long to get to the point;

- When we feel deadline pressure that causes us to cut someone off;

- When the speaker has a long track record of "overtalking";

- When we are sure that our idea is superior and therefore must be heard right now;

- When we are enthusiastic about what the other person is saying and we can't wait to jump in.

All of these are understandable, and all of us are guilty of one or more of these infractions. We justify our behavior by our busy calendars, stretched resources, and maybe even low blood sugar from missing lunch. But *all* of the examples above, even the last one, are examples of uncivil behavior. We don't mean to be rude. We may not even realize we are being rude. In fact, if the other person seemed offended we might be surprised and even consider him to be overly sensitive. But ask yourself this question: If the roles were reversed, would you feel hurt, slighted, or even a little ticked off if someone cut you off or presumed to know your thoughts so well they could finish your sentence? Remember, there is often a disconnect between what the offender and the offendee deem to be hurtful.

For more patient listening:

> Step 1: Build self-awareness. What or who causes me to listen impatiently?

> Step 2: Practice self-management. Deepen and slow your breath to calm yourself. Stay in the moment. Be other-conscious but self-aware. Address the cause of your impatience with the other person if and when you can.

Managing Emotional Triggers

This is good place to talk once again about triggers and trigger moments, those seemingly random occurrences that push our buttons and send us into orbit. For example, do any of these sound familiar?

- "When I got that voicemail message from Nicholas yesterday, I got so mad I couldn't see straight! Honestly, it's a good thing he wasn't in the office because I don't think I could have held my tongue."

- "Did you hear what happened? When Matt confronted Kim with the monthly results she was like a deer in the headlights. She just stood there, staring at the paper, not saying a word."

- "I don't know what happened. It felt like my presentation was going well, and then I saw Carol come into the back of the room and my mind went completely blank."

We've all experienced moments like these where our hearts pound, our faces get red, our palms get sweaty, and we can't think straight. These moments seem random and unexpected, but they aren't. Each of us responds to certain triggers, which in turn set off the physical and mental responses described above. Daniel Goleman[13] aptly refers to these moments as "amygdala hijacks." This is when the amygdala (the emotional center of the brain), responding to a flood of stress hormones, basically hijacks the cerebral cortex (the thinking part of the brain) so that we don't waste valuable time and energy thinking, allowing the body to save itself and run away. This was a critical survival mechanism in our prehistoric ancestors.

Imagine this: Our long-distant forebear walks out of his cave and sees a saber-tooth tiger crouched right outside. Suppose he pauses for a moment to think, "Hmm ... that's a really large tiger and this is not my largest club. I will probably need my bigger club and will have to swing it with 25 percent more force." And the tiger enjoys a nice caveman dinner.

We are genetically linked to the ones who lived, and therefore we all inherited the same brain wiring which causes fight, flight, or freeze. So, with no time to think, our caveman ancestors would either pull a sudden surprise attack on the tiger so it would run away (fight), run back into the safety of the cave (flight), or hold very still and hope the tiger would not notice them (freeze).

Today when we perceive a danger or threat, our brains still go into survival mode. We can't help it. It's the way we are wired. So don't blame yourself for the fact that your mind goes blank at these moments. Accept that this is just your brain being your brain, and then learn how to handle your trigger moments.

Let's start with the body. The first thing you've probably noticed is one or more of the following physiological responses:

- ➲ Rapid heart rate

- ➲ Shallow breathing

- ➲ Red face

- ➲ Sweaty palms

- ➲ Butterflies in the tummy

- ➲ Tension in legs or shoulders

- ➲ Narrowing of vision field

This is your safety mechanism at work. Your body is literally preparing you to run away or to fight in defense of yourself. And when you experience that totally blank mind, it's because your amygdala has hijacked your brain so you don't endanger yourself by thinking too much.

Uh-oh.

That's right. Just at that moment when you *really* need a clear head and crisp thinking, your brain does the exact opposite when triggered by the presence of stress hormones.

But wait. It gets worse. The more severe the "hijacking," the longer it takes to recover your full mental capacities. Research shows that it can take as long as twenty to thirty minutes for the thinking part of the brain to re-engage after a hijack. So if you've ever been triggered and you took a walk around the block or around the parking lot to settle down, you might recall that it took awhile before you felt fully in control of your wits. (In mid-town Manhattan, it takes exactly twenty minutes to walk around the block. Trust me. I know!)

Can you shorten that recovery time? Even better, can you avoid the hijack altogether?

Yes, you can.

Your body's physiological responses are, in fact, an early warning system that alerts you when you are heading for the edge. For me, when I feel my breath get shallow and my face flush, I'm on the potential path to shutdown. At that point I deliberately stop whatever I'm doing and take two long, slow, deep breaths, which slows my heart rate and signals my brain that this "tiger" I'm facing isn't really going to eat me, and if I stay calm and present, I can work through this challenging moment. Yes, it is that simple: just start with two or three long, slow, deep breaths. The body's response on both a physical and neurological level is complex...yet predictable.

Jessica and Mark from Chapter One were both suffering from "amygdala hijack" when the stress built up and they reacted without thinking. If they had recognized that they were in a very emotional state, they could have gotten control by following the steps below. You can too. Remember:

1. Stop! Before you engage in fight, flight or freeze, stop and get yourself together;

2. Breathe! Take at least two long, slow, deep breaths and keep the rational part of your brain fully oxygenated. This will also slow your heart rate.

3. Think! Be mindful. Be very aware of the emotions you are feeling and manage those first, *then* start to manage the situation.

4. Act. Once you are calm, find a positive action as opposed to a negative reaction.

You're probably thinking, "But wait a minute! How can I have the presence of mind to remember and perform these four steps when my rational brain is temporarily disconnected?"

Here's how:

- First, when you catch yourself in the moment, your thinking is not yet totally disabled, so you can still grab the useful thought which is: Breathe!

- Second, if you've prepared yourself before the trigger moment or event occurs, you know (1) what your hot buttons are, and (2) how to spot the early warning signs that you're heading for the edge. In other words, you are alert to the possibility of danger before going into full-blown hijack.

- Finally, you can implement the four steps to return to a calm and present state and avert disaster before it occurs. Let's prepare now.

ACTIVITY

Know-Thyself Activity

Who or what is your "saber-tooth tiger" at work? When do you feel the urge to fight, fly, or freeze?

My trigger moments are:

_____

_____

_____

_____

_____

What happens to you physically when confronted with one of your triggers? What do you notice about your body when you're scared, angry, or unhappily surprised?

My body signals are:

_____

_____

_____

_____

_____

Remember, those body signals are your early warning that trouble could be brewing in your brain. If you want to get ahead of the tiger, you have to pick up those signals.

Now, think back to a time in your recent past when you reacted instead of responded. In addition to your body's reaction, what were you feeling emotionally at the time? What was stirred up for you?

Emotionally, I was feeling:

_____

_____

_____

_____

_____

Can you remember other times when you reacted instead of responded? Can you recall feeling these same emotions? Do you remember what triggered these reactions? Is there a pattern here?

If you are noticing a pattern, ask yourself what deeply held belief or value is being threatened or ignored in these situations. We all have certain ideals that we perceive to be fundamental, and *we all believe that our own values are the right ones*. But we don't all share the same values hierarchy. Our values come from the different societies that influenced our development: our family, our circle of friends, our university, our church, our country, and so forth. Looking back at Jessica and Mark, it is likely that Jessica has a deeply held value centered on being thoughtful or polite, while Mark may hold a core value centered on efficiency or goal attainment. Whether they realized it or not, both were triggered emotionally when they felt their values were being overlooked or threatened.

> *When you feel yourself react emotionally, ask yourself what value is being threatened or overlooked.*

Back to the activity. Now, while you are calm, think of how you can manage those emotions so that you can then handle challenging situations most effectively.

My recent "moment of personal regret" was:

_____

_____

_____

_____

The trigger was:

_____

_____

_____

_____

The emotions I felt at the time were:

_____

_____

_____

It was typical/atypical for me to feel those emotions in this situation because:

_____

_____

_____

My values that felt threatened or overlooked were:

_____

_____

_____

In the future, I will manage those emotions by:

_____

_____

_____

If you've taken the time to really think through this activity, you have taken some giant steps toward better self-management, and in turn, toward fewer moments of personal regret.

◆

Revisiting Ron and Sara

Remember Ron, the bright but long-winded strategist? There's no question that he is smart and dedicated, but he is undermining his own effectiveness because the truth is that everyone knows Ron overtalks; everyone, that is, except Ron. This is where we scratch our heads and ask, "How is that possible? How can he *not* know when every single meeting he's in runs over?"

The fact is that Ron doesn't associate his verbosity with meeting duration. In his view, meetings run long for lots of reasons that have nothing to do with him. And even though Ron overtalks in other settings, people's chief complaint to his boss, Irene, have to do with meetings running long. Irene has told Ron more than once that there are complaints and his meetings cannot run over, but she did not specifically mention the issue of his verbosity. "I assumed he was smart enough to figure out what the problem was," she told me. So what did Ron do? He took Irene's feedback as given and focused on running efficient meetings. From then on he always used an agenda, started and ended on time, and kept the number of agenda items to a reasonable level. Good actions, but missing the point. Without very *specific* feedback, Ron didn't know what to fix so he kept right on overtalking, but at least he ended meetings at the scheduled time.

Ron needs to focus on overtalking, but first he needs to be made aware of the specific problem. How would you coach him so he can be more self-aware and make better choices?

_____

_____

_____

Ron doesn't just overtalk in meetings at work. He overtalks all the time, including in his sessions with me. In our first session, it took him five minutes to answer a simple question. I surreptitiously timed him using the clock behind him. After he had finished, I told him that I had timed him and asked him how long he thought he had spoken. He said, "About a minute and a half, maybe two minutes." When I told him it was five minutes, he said, "Oh, that doesn't surprise me. I know I talk too much. My wife teases me about it and calls me 'the professor' when I do this at home." This was actually good news and bad news. Ron was aware of the problem, but he was not aware of the *impact* of the problem on his colleagues, nor did he have any idea of how to change his behavior.

Overtalking is a common problem that has a devastating impact in our time-crunched work environment. Even so, it's hard for some people to leave out what they consider to be important details, or to cut short a lively and productive discussion, or to stick to the point and not go off on tangents. They don't realize that their attempts to be thorough just end up being confusing. The finesse here is knowing how much detail or discussion is enough; savvy leaders manage their own messages and pay attention to clues from others to ensure topics get just enough coverage.

First, Ron needed to understand that the impact is significant and addressing it was vital to his future success. Once that was clear, he needed to dramatically increase his self-awareness regarding verbal tangents, so he bought a little hand-held voice recorder, recorded his side of various phone conversations and listened to them during his commute so he could hear when and how he rambled. This way he could catch himself and, over time, begin to self-correct.

I worked with Ron to learn and practice new behaviors, such as:

- ➲ Preparing his talking points in advance, practicing with a stopwatch, and trimming out the excess verbiage;

- ➲ Noticing when he goes off on tangents, however interesting they are to him, and getting back to the point quickly and seamlessly;

- ➲ Being more *other-aware* in meetings and looking for nonverbal cues that people are ready to move on. In other words, getting out of his head and staying in the room;

- ➲ Keeping his watch or cell phone clock in front of him at meetings and limiting his verbal contributions to three minutes or less;

- ➲ Using questions to encourage others to talk, and strive for a ratio where others do more talking than he does;

- ➲ Asking for feedback from his boss and others regarding his progress.

Ron was able to dramatically decrease the amount of excess verbiage in his everyday speech and in his prepared remarks. He knew he might slip back on occasion, so he courageously asked two of his trusted colleagues to give him feedback in the moment if they noticed him going off on tangents.

Now go back and look at the case study of Sara. How can Sara better manage her moments? What specific behaviors must she become aware of so that she can change?

_____

_____

_____

Now, how would you deliver this feedback to Sara to help her understand exactly what to change, and why?

_____

_____

_____

Sara is motivated and optimistic and her boss believes she will take the feedback well. Simply and directly, he told her about her habitual behaviors and the impact they were having on how senior people perceived her. He reminded her of her professional goals as well as all the hard work she was doing to achieve them. Then, he offered her support through coaching to address the behaviors. Sara understood immediately that he was trying to help her create a more powerful future and was completely open to coaching. My goal was to help her see herself as a more mature, strong, and capable professional and then work with her to create the behavioral data points that would support that image, starting with a few simple behaviors. She must:

➲ Sit up straight in meetings, arms and hands resting on the conference table, and keep her hands away from her hair. When she catches herself twirling, she must simply drop her hands back to "home base," which is a comfortable, hand-neutral position on the table;

⮑ Pay attention to when she tilts her head, both at work and outside work. If she is not aware of when she does it, she must ask a trusted colleague to signal her so she can correct it in the moment;

⮑ Use the slightly deeper stronger tones in her voice to sound more confident and mature;

⮑ On meeting days, add a tailored jacket to her usual skirt and blouse attire;

⮑ Come to each meeting ready to contribute. She must prepare her thoughts in advance and speak them in a firm voice at a measured pace. She must avoid youthful fillers such as "like" and "you know" and use stronger phrases such as "I believe" and "our research clearly showed."

Once Sara knew what to do, she easily assimilated the above into her work behavior, although the hardest habit to break was not the hair twirl; it was the head tilt. But even that has gotten better over time, thanks to greater self-awareness and self-management.

MOMENT TO
REFLECT

- ❑ What you don't know *can* hurt you. Get clear on your strengths and potential weaknesses.

- ❑ Self-awareness is a precondition to being present, while self-consciousness is a distraction.

- ❑ Listening patiently is a skill worth developing.

- ❑ Certain triggers can cause a "fight-or-flight" response that hinders the ability to think clearly under pressure.

- ❑ When it comes to unconscious but annoying habits, most people would rather know about them so they can address them.

- ❑ To be fully present, you need to get out of your head and into the room.

4

IT'S ALL ABOUT THEM

Alec gave himself a little pep talk on his way to the Monday morning staff meeting. Sure, things at the firm had been difficult lately. Deal flow was slowing again, which meant some belt tightening. On the other hand, there were glimmers of potential business coming into the pipeline. He decided to avoid any "doom and gloom" discussion at today's meetings and focus on the positive. He didn't want people to get all upset for nothing, and he knew he didn't have the energy right now to handle it if they did.

Alec made an effort to smile at the team as he took his seat at the head of the conference table and started right away with the first item on the agenda. As the meeting progressed, people started exchanging concerned looks. In spite of his carefully selecting neutral words, it was obvious to everyone that Alec was uncomfortable. What was going on? They noticed that he kept pulling his collar away from his neck and twisting his head back and forth as if his shirt were two sizes too small. His shoulders were hunched and his face looked pained. The team exchanged more worried glances and wondered, "Should we be prepared for the worst? What was he not telling us? Is this the end?"

Alec closed the brief meeting with a few words of encouragement to everyone that brighter days were ahead and walked back to his office thinking, "Okay, I guess that went pretty well." So imagine his surprise when one of the firm's best and brightest sales managers walked into his office an hour later and asked if she should start sending out her resume.

◆

What are your observations regarding Alec and the meeting? What really happened?

_____

_____

_____

If you said anything about mixed messages, subtext, or zero self-awareness, you are right on track. In our coaching session a few days later Alec told me about the meeting and his shock over the sales manager's reaction. I asked him to take a step back and try to remember what his goal was for that difficult meeting. After some thought he said, "Just to get through it." That was a very weak position and gave him nothing—no goal, no compass point—to guide him through what was, for him, a deceptively challenging situation. He forgot a key element in his planning:

> *For every interaction related to something important, be clear on your purpose and plan your approach in advance.*

We mentioned the idea of connecting to your purpose in Chapter Two and will discuss it in more detail in Chapter Five since it relates to how one prepares to communicate. For now, let's stay focused on Alec and the things we discussed in his coaching session.

⮑ At the beginning of our session, Alec insisted that he was able to remain neutral in the staff meeting and pooh-poohed the idea that he telegraphed his feelings of discomfort quite clearly. Then I pointed out that bits of evidence to the contrary were still leaking out as he told me about the meeting, and he finally admitted that he was not being honest with himself about his feelings on the day of the meeting or even today in our session. In retrospect he realized there was a serious disconnect between what he was feeling (doubt, fear) and what he was saying ("all will be well"). I reminded Alec that when the message is mixed, our body language is picked up more strongly than our actual words. So his real feelings came through loud and clear, and because he was unaware of how he was coming across, he couldn't manage the moment.

⮑ He was also unaware of what was going on in the room: he missed people's nonverbal distress signals, didn't open the meeting up for questions or discussion, and rushed away afterwards because he felt so overwhelmed. So of course he was blindsided by what happened later. He missed every clue.

➲ Alec admitted that he was basically pretending that everything was fine because he didn't have the energy to deal with other people's potential upset. What he didn't realize is that it takes even more energy to mask emotions than to express them.[14]

➲ Because he made it "all about him" instead of "all about them," he missed a real opportunity to connect with his people on a human level. He was entirely self-focused because of his anxiety. We understand this. But if he'd been honest with himself about what he was feeling, he could have used the moment to share his own fears and trepidations and ask them about theirs.[15] Then they could have had a genuine open discussion, separating facts from assumptions, reminding themselves about potential, and maybe even rallying themselves. Instead, Alec went to the very common default position of "no crying in baseball" and lobbed a mixed-message grenade that almost blew up in his face.

➲ Alec also fell into a familiar trap of underestimating people's understanding of the real conditions faced by the firm and their need for transparent communication. Many leaders mistakenly assume people know less than they really do. Without that realization, and without a positive or constructive purpose for the meeting, Alec was like a ship without rudder or destination. He could not steer the discussion to a productive outcome.

With 20-20 hindsight, Alec realized that his goal for the meeting should have been to have an open discussion about both the opportunities and the realities facing the business. His approach could have been to share some of his own feelings and use open-ended questions to allow people to share their thoughts and feelings. He decided to set a goal that next time he would stay in the room, physically and emotionally, until everyone had a chance to say what was on his or her mind.

PREMISE #7

Presence Is Only "Presence" if You Are With Other People!

And by "with" I mean in the same room or the same building, or on the same video conference, or part of the same string of e-mails. If they can see you, hear you, or read your words, presence matters.

It's easy to get presence just right when you are by yourself or when you rehearse a conversation in your imagination. We are all perfectly behaved in The Land of Would (as in "Here's what I would do in that situation..."). The problem is no one lives in that land. We usually live in The Land of Did, and it's likely that whatever we "did" was done with, to, or in front of, other people. In his head, Alec delivered his comments cleanly and with no emotion. *In the room...* not so much.

So, this chapter is about what shows up to them when you show up—and they *are* watching. Work is not easy, and we are imperfect humans struggling to manage imperfect situations, which is why you need to know:

What Shows Up When You Show Up?

What shows up when you show up on a good day, bad day, or "nothing" day? Do you know? Or do you just think you know? And do you know how your moods and subsequent behavior impact other people, regardless of your intent?

There are dozens of books, webinars, classes, and so forth devoted to various aspects of interpersonal effectiveness. Our model focuses on a subset of interpersonal skills and behaviors that impact, and are impacted by, your presence.

Interpersonal Skills: The Model

Interpersonal Skills and Presence:

- ➲ Building rapport

- ➲ Mirroring

- ➲ Building trust

- ➲ Accurately gauging others' feelings and reactions

- ➲ Consciously managing to the context

- ➲ Listening to build bridges

Building Rapport

Presence is about connecting, so rapport is a good skill to have. Have you ever been on an airplane and found yourself in a surprisingly entertaining conversation with the stranger next to you? Did you find yourself laughing at similar experiences after only a few minutes or even confiding something rather personal after only a few hours? It's rare indeed to hit it off with someone you've never met before, and what really strikes me is how quickly rapport can be established. One of my favorite encounters was a trip when my seat neighbor and I were both exhausted, and after a perfunctory hello, we agreed neither would take offense if we ignored each other during the flight. I focused on some work and she went to sleep until we were interrupted by the dinner service. We cautiously exchanged a few words about the meal and the next thing we knew, two hours had passed and Annie and I were still yakking it up like old pals. We exchanged cards at the end of the flight, laughing about how our earlier resolve to not talk turned into nearly three hours of intense conversation. "How did *that* happen?" we wondered.

Good question. Why do we feel an instant affinity for some folks and not for others? How does rapport grow? And what does this have to do with presence?

In his book *Social Intelligence* author Daniel Goleman shares "the recipe for rapport" as he learned it from his Harvard professor Robert Rosenthal. According to Rosenthal, the special connection of rapport always involves three elements: "mutual attention, shared positive feeling, and a well-coordinated nonverbal duet."[16] That seems to explain what happened with Annie and me pretty well. The "shared positive feeling" was, at first, the feeling of relief that our seatmate would respect our desire for quiet. The "well-coordinated nonverbal duet" was the cautious way we initiated the conversation over dinner. I remember clearly that we glanced at each other to check for openness, and we spoke in lowered voices so as not to appear too obtrusive to the other. Gently, gradually, and together, we increased our eye contact and the pace of our speech which, in turn, signaled the start of rapport and allowed us to each introduce more personal conversational content.

Goleman goes on to point out that the first element—mutual attention—is especially meaningful to us because both parties *experience being experienced.* There are few things more powerful than when we know we are being truly and deeply heard by someone else whose attention is fully on us. Once Annie and I made the decision to connect, we definitely had "the experience of being experienced." Maybe that's why some of those initial high-rapport conversations happen on airplanes: no IMs or cell phones to distract us, no one knocking on the door for our attention, and the white noise of the engines to create a little cocoon of privacy. For those moments, each of us is 100 percent present, and that's a rare and wonderful thing.

How about virtual rapport? There's no doubt that it's more difficult to find the time, energy, or opportunity to build rapport when many meetings are virtual. Fran Milnes, head of marketing, AMACO Region, Novartis shared this tip: "As we no longer enter and leave physical rooms where natural small talk occurs, a scheduled check-in allows people to arrive, settle in, and engage in small talk. I like to kick off the check-in with a topic like 'something interesting you have read.' I can see my people forming stronger bonds over a newly discovered shared experience."

Think about the people at work with whom you share a special rapport. Are there a few that you really connect with? Of course you work well with all of the people in your group, but are there a few where the communication is easier, the decisions faster, the meetings more fun? Do you feel as if these folks and you "speak the same language" or are "on the same page," and do find you actually like these people more than some others, and you're not sure why? Goleman says that when people share rapport, they can be more creative together and more efficient in decision making. Is that consistent with your experience?

Now ask yourself: *How* did you and your colleagues build that rapport? Maybe it was on an airplane, but most likely it was not, so how did it happen, and what conditions were in place that allowed you two to build rapport?

_____

_____

_____

Is it possible to replicate that result with someone else? What conditions would need to be in place for you to have the *opportunity* to build rapport with other colleagues?

_____

_____

_____

Was that last question difficult? Some people have trouble articulating the conditions that would have to be in place. If you struggled, let's approach it from the opposite direction: What obstacles get in the way of meeting new people or building stronger relationships at work? For instance, do you:

- ❑ Eat lunch at your desk to catch up on e-mails?
- ❑ Rush from meeting to meeting, arriving or logging in just in time for each one?

❑ Send an e-mail to a colleague down the hall rather than dropping in?

❑ Show up late to conference calls, or turn off your camera during videoconferences so you can multitask?

❑ Spend the "really big meeting" coffee break checking your messages instead of chatting with other meeting attendees?

❑ Sit in the same spot with the same people at group events such as town hall meetings?

If you checked even one box on that list, you are creating the perfect conditions—for solitude and separateness. You are missing opportunities to build rapport. Hey, I know how it is. During my years working inside big corporations, I could have checked every box too, sometimes all in the same week. In fact, eating at my desk and pushing through emails before the start of meetings slowly became my default position until I realized that getting caught up on a few e-mails came with a very high price tag: fewer stimulating and nourishing relationships, and way too much "alone time" for an extrovert. Not a good way to develop strong presence, is it?

For rapport to grow, the conditions have to be right. To find the common ground, we actually have to have conversations with people that allow us to discover our shared likes, dislikes, hopes and fears. To have conversations, you need to find fifteen minutes, or even five minutes, to engage in some small talk, even on conference calls. Back in my busy corporate days, once I realized my old cloistered pattern, I made a special effort to space my meetings out a bit so I could prepare for the next meeting, and then arrive a little early and engage in small talk before the meeting started. It helped me recharge my extrovert battery, and as a bonus I also strengthened and reinforced my network.

To find common ground, we also have to be willing to reveal things about ourselves that give people something to respond to. For instance, some folks share through the choices they make to decorate their offices or cubicles, displaying ball caps with their favorite team's logo, or watercolors from their child's art class. Some put photos from vacations, weddings, or family events. I used to keep a framed head shot of my gorgeous German shepherd in my office because dog lovers would respond to her immediately, and we could start to build rapport that way. Whatever you choose, let it say something about who you are as a person, and when people ask about it, be ready to engage in a little small talk.

Finally, up-and-comers often tell me that they have to influence others over whom they have no direct control. "In order to have the means to influence others," say authors Ed Keller and Brad Fay in *The Face-to-Face Book*, "a person needs to be in touch regularly with other people. You can be the most knowledgeable person in the world about a particular topic, but if you are a loner and don't interact with others very often it is hard for your ideas to spread."[17] To be known, you must be seen and heard.

MINIACTIVITY

Unless you work virtually and your company has a travel restriction, everything on that obstacle/opportunity list is 100 percent within your control. What will you do differently? Write a positive intention for yourself starting with the words: "I will create more opportunities to connect with others by (list your actions):

_____

_____

_____

Why should you make this effort? What's the potential upside for you and/or your teammates if you do?

_____

_____

_____

◆

Mirroring

I worked in midtown Manhattan for many years. Specifically, I worked at Rockefeller Center, close to Saint Patrick's Cathedral, Saks Fifth Avenue, the Today Show, and the skating rink. Most days the sidewalks are packed with busy New Yorkers hurrying to their next destination, as well as strolling tourists taking in all the world-famous sights. It is extremely common to be crossing the street in an elbow-to-elbow crowd and encounter someone coming right at you from the opposite side. Then comes the little dance: we both step to one side, and then we both step to the other side. You've done this, right? I call it the midtown mambo, which is a duet performed by two strangers who are *not* having a good time! Well, a few years ago I decided to try a little experiment. Every time I found myself doing the midtown mambo with a fellow pedestrian, I would look him or her in the face and give a huge smile, as if to say, "Isn't this a crazy place?" And guess what? The other pedestrian always smiled back. That's what I wanted to find out. They smiled back. Why? Because of that flash of shared understanding, in that split second we acknowledged New York is a crazy place and we chose to be there, and the little dance was all part of the experience, and then we went on our way. It's a fabulous New York moment, and it's an example of mirroring.

Mirroring is when one person's body language reflects another person's body language. We used to teach mirroring to salespeople as a way to subtly establish rapport with the buyer. The idea was that if the prospect was sitting in a certain way, say with their legs crossed, the salesperson should sit in a mirror image of that, sending an unconscious signal that we are alike. However, as the technique became more widespread (and less subtle) people sensed what was going on and quite rightly felt manipulated, so we don't encourage deliberate mimicry any more. What we do teach is the fact that mirroring happens naturally when two people really are in synch with each other. Research shows that people will very naturally mimic each other's facial expressions, gestures, posture, vocal melody, and pace. But it only happens when we allow ourselves the time, energy and focus to actually *look* at the other person and *listen* to him or her. If we don't pick up the cues, we can't participate in the dance. In other words, once again, we have to be *fully present*.

"Tempo rhythm" is a form of mirroring. It is a term used to describe a person's natural "beat" or "tempo." Some people have a naturally fast tempo—they talk fast, walk fast, drive fast—while others have a slower natural tempo. We can and do vary our preferred rhythm when the situation calls for it. When we consciously slow down to walk with another person at his tempo, or when we speed up our talking to match our conversation partner, we are mirroring his pace in order to stay connected. Many of us do this unconsciously. Research tells us that the more rapport that exists between two people, the more they mimic each other's timing, facial expressions, speech patterns, and gestures. Have you noticed that?

Building Trust

In our seminars, when we ask people to define trust, there's a long silence as participants pause to think about how exactly to explain something as esoteric as trust. But if we ask how trust is built, they answer more quickly. If we ask how trust is destroyed, they answer even more quickly—and vehemently. This is another one of those instances in which we may not know exactly what something is, but we know it when we see it.

What do you think? What is trust, and how is trust built? What helps and what hurts a trusting relationship?

Let's start with a dictionary definition:

---

trust /truhst/   Adapted from Dictionary.com

Verb:

1. To rely on the integrity, strength, ability, surety, and so forth, of a person or thing. For example: *We can trust their recommendation since they are experts in their field.*

2. To have confident expectation of something; hope. For example: *We trust that the banquet will exceed your expectations.*

3. To rely on a person or thing. For example: *I trust him to keep his promise.*

When there is trust, we know we can rely on the other person and believe she will meet our expectations. Of course, building trust takes time and attention. Consider the story of Georgia:

Georgia is a senior auditor in internal controls with more than fifteen years of experience. She manages a team of auditors whose job it is to review workflow processes and financial reporting for their assigned business unit, the product development department, to ensure legal and regulatory compliance. When Georgia and her team do their jobs well, they uncover potential problems, bring them to the attention of the business, and recommend solutions. In their eyes, they prevent serious trouble and are genuinely trying to help the business.

Their customers don't see it that way. To the people in product development, going through an audit is a big hassle in which they have to constantly interrupt their regular work to justify everything they do. While this is a natural tension that the auditors have to learn to deal with, it can be disheartening when no one is ever happy to see you coming.

As a long-time audit professional, Georgia understands this dynamic and is supportive and encouraging with her team. She coaches her auditors to build strong, trusting relationships with the folks in product development by interacting with them outside the audit period in division-wide meetings and networking events. She encourages them to learn as much as they can about "the business of the business" including the strategy, goals, and vision. She also expects them to be transparent about the audit process so that the business really understands and buys into the audit process. Finally, she takes every opportunity to remind folks on both sides that they have the same end goal.

What do you notice about the coaching Georgia is giving to her people?

_____

_____

_____

Georgia's focus in developing her team is to build their interpersonal skills. She knows she can't change the natural tension between auditors and auditees, but she also knows that strong, trusting relationships between the teams will make things easier for everyone and result in the best outcome. Georgia's coaching is targeted to four aspects of trust and their supporting behaviors:

1. Credibility, demonstrated through knowledge of the product development business as well as their own business

2. Transparency, demonstrated by openly sharing the what, how, and why of each audit

3. Rapport, built through non-audit interaction

4. Common focus, built through dedication to a shared goal

What do you think is the impact of these skills and behaviors on the auditors' presence?

_____

_____

_____

Yes, the auditors will feel more confident and less self-conscious when there is more rapport and trust between them and their colleagues in product development. If they are more relaxed and natural, their auditees will feel the same way.

Accurately Gauging Their Reactions

Imagine for a moment the last in-person meeting you attended. Remember who was there, and where they sat? You don't need to remember every topic that was covered, just the general gist of things. Now, can you recall any time at that meeting when people had an emotional response to something that was said (or implied) during the meeting? If so, what specifically did you notice about other people's responses?

⊃   Who smiled at whom? Or who frowned at whom?

⊃   Who suddenly sat forward, or sat back, and when?

⊃   Who folded their arms at some point in the discussion? Were their arms folded loosely or tightly?

⊃   Whose voice became noticeably louder, or softer?

⊃   Did anyone sigh audibly?

⊃   What else?

When I coach people who need to be more adept at noticing the subtle signals in a room, I send them on a "subtext safari." I ask them to come back to our next session with a list of the specific things they noticed, like the list above. Just make a list of what you notice without any interpretation. Why? Because I want them to start to train their eyes and ears to pay attention. When you pay attention, you begin to realize that there's an awful lot of unspoken communication going on in any meeting. The problem is we are usually too distracted by the topic, or by time pressure, or by our thoughts, or even by our growling stomachs to pay close attention to these valuable clues. If you are the leader (meeting leader, team leader, etc.) it is up to you to notice, because the nonverbal stuff is really good information that you need to be an effective leader. Being fully present means getting out of your head and into the room, noticing and, if needed, flexing and responding.

Being "in the room" includes the virtual rooms we visit every day thanks to videoconferencing. Yes, it is more difficult to pick up on non-verbal cues during virtual meetings. People may not have their cameras on, and microphones distort the voice so that the subtleties may be lost. In addition, technology limitations may cause us to unintentionally talk over each other, thereby losing some of what was said. And the larger the onscreen group, the less likely people are to participate, meaning fewer clues for you.

When you do pick up those clues, how accurate are you at interpreting them? How well can you translate that subtext into what people are actually thinking or feeling so that you know how to manage the moment? And how do you know if you are right? (Because if you are the leader, people might be too intimidated by you or by the group to "call you out" and correct you, or tell you that you misunderstood them.)

Here's a technique we use all the time in classes and meetings that opens the door for people to tell you what's on their minds.

Name It and Frame It Technique

One day, my wonderful colleague Diana Hird and I were collaborating on a concept for one of our presence classes that would give presenters a different but effective way to uncover subtext in a class. Here's what we came up with, and it really works.

> "Name it and Frame it" is a technique that a meeting leader or presenter can use when they spot some sort of subtext going on in the room and they suspect there is something more that needs discussing. It has two parts:

⊃ Name it—refers to the specific subtext item that the presenter noticed: A frown, a smile, a sigh, and so forth. Be sure to "name" only the physical manifestation and not an interpretation of it. For instance, "I see you're frowning" is the observation versus "That seemed to make you mad," your interpretation. Just stick with the observation.

⊃ Frame it—refers to the open-ended question the presenter uses to invite the participant to share his thoughts or feelings. In other words, the presenter offers the frame and allows the other person to "color in the picture" herself.

⊃ Together, Name it and Frame it sounds something like this:

- Sally, I noticed that made you smile. What were you thinking?

- Oh Toni, that was a deep sigh! What's on your mind?

- Gerry, you're frowning right now. What's up?

➲ Name it and Frame it does *not* sound like this:

- Oh Carlos, why do you frown every time I make a suggestion?

- Jack, you folded your arms when I said that. Do you disagree?

- Sandy, for heaven's sake, if you have something to say, say it!

- Tim, I noticed you sat up when we mentioned Atlanta. Did you finally wake up?

Of course you're not going to use the Name it and Frame it technique every time you spot subtext. The best time to use it is when you see that someone has something to say, but he is holding back from saying it, and you believe the group would benefit from hearing what the participant has to say. Name it and Frame it is an invitation to say it. The participant can choose to answer or not answer, but our experience is that people will answer more often than not, especially if the environment is one of relatively high trust and if the leader doesn't employ the technique as a test or a "gotcha."

Name it and Frame it is much more difficult in larger virtual meetings. If you do notice something, it is better to take it offline and speak to the person directly right after the meeting.

What do you think is the impact on the leader's presence when they use Name it and Frame it effectively?

_____

_____

_____

_____

Right. They demonstrate that they are "in the room," that they are ready and willing to listen, and that they care about what people are thinking. It keeps them connected to the group, demonstrates courage and caring, and engages the group so it is not a one-way discussion.

Consciously Managing to the Context

In Chapter Two you learned that you are better able to manage your presence when you have a pre-sense of two things: (1) How you come across, and (2) What others expect of you. We spent time on the first part—how you come across—and the importance on managing subtext in Chapter Two. Now let's talk about the second part—the context—because what others expect of you depends on the context, and that context shifts all the time. Let me show you.

As you can see in the diagram below, there you are in the center. This is you with all of your unique skills, talents, experiences, passions, and personality. But at work, you exist within the context of your role or your level, which exists within the context of your function or department, which in turn exists within the context of your company or your community.

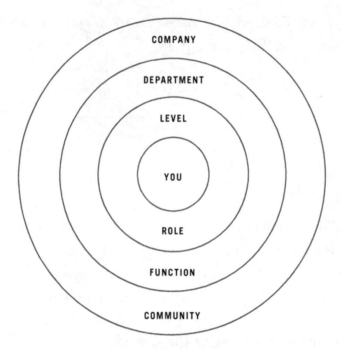

There are other subcontexts we could add too, because your role shifts even in the course of a typical day. You might be the leader at your 9:00 AM meeting, the subject matter expert at your 11:00 AM meeting, and the empathetic boss at your 2:00 PM meeting. We all have to shift how we play each role as the context changes in order to ensure we accomplish the goal and meet others' expectations. The good news is that most of us do this pretty seamlessly all day long without really thinking about it. When we discuss this in classes or coaching, people are usually surprised at how much they shift throughout the day without consciously planning it. Now I ask you: Is it possible that you could increase your effectiveness by being more mindful of context and the related expectations as you move through your day? Consider this story:

> *A few years ago I was asked to do some presence coaching*
> *for Greg, a former salesperson, who was relocated from the*

Midwest to the head office in New York and promoted to a marketing director position. Greg is a very smart and high-spirited guy, but brains and personality were not going to be enough to jump-start him in his new job. To be successful he had to shift his thinking about himself and the way that others would now view him. He had to acknowledge the multiple, dramatic changes of context: first, from his old "Wild West" field sales community to the more constrained and formal head office community, and second, from his mostly individual contributor role to a new role where he was a higher-level manager of managers. In my first conversation with him he said he knew it was going to be an adjustment to move to New York and to work in the head office, but he felt he got the hang of that fairly quickly. He was partly correct. Greg spent a lot of time preparing to perform his new responsibilities, but hadn't spent any time thinking about the expectations people would have of him because of his new level, or function, or community. In fact, he was very surprised when I mentioned how people might change their interactions with him because of his level. "I don't believe in all that hierarchical crap," he said. "In sales, no one cares about level, they care about results." Well, that may be true in the field, but in the head office of this particular company they care a lot about level. People work hard for years to climb each rung of that ladder, and things like title mean everything to them. If Greg wasn't careful, he was going to insult a few people and disappoint some others because of their expectations around level.

◆

Levels and titles matter, depending on the company, industry, or even the country. Titles carry a lot of weight internally for some functions, or externally for others, or even not at all for others.

What do you think about Greg's situation? His context is now an environment where levels and titles matter. What might you say to help him understand this?

_____

_____

_____

Greg needs to understand that in this company, titles are linked very strongly in people's minds with achievement. To recognize the title is to recognize the achievement. Likewise, to have disdain for titles can send an unintended message that you don't respect the person or his achievement. His head office colleagues are used to people behaving in a certain way because of the hierarchy. If he wants to be effective, he needs to pay attention to the way things work in the new environment and adapt his behavior accordingly. And by the way, there are folks in the head office who've already decided that Greg can't be effective because he came from sales. Is that fair? Of course not. But people have expectations of us simply because we have a certain role or function, fair or unfair. For instance, in our classes we often have people from different functions. We ask everyone: What expectations do people have of you, fair or unfair, because you are a specialist in your field? For instance, we ask the corporate attorneys what folks expect of them, fair or unfair, because they are attorneys, and they answer: "People expect us to know every law ever written in every jurisdiction, and occasionally someone asks if we can get them out of a parking ticket." Really! We ask the accountants too, who answer:

"People expect us to be good with numbers and very boring." How about you, marketer? "People don't think we work very hard and yet they expect us to be brilliantly creative all of the time." Recently I had a woman in my class who laughingly described herself as unique because she is "an actuary with a personality." People are often quite funny when they share the silly stereotypes that others ascribe to their professions. And we laugh because we know these stereotypes exist, although most stereotyping isn't funny.

What do these stereotypes have to do with presence? Consider this story:

> *Bettina is a human resources director with a brusque, somewhat impersonal communication style. She's a strong leader. Under her direction, the HR team successfully implemented numerous programs benefiting staff and managers over the years, including helping the company gain recognition on one of those prestigious Best Places to Work lists. But people were frustrated with Bettina. They complained that she was uncaring and dismissive. In fact, on her most current 360° feedback report, one person wrote, "Where is the 'human' in our Human Resources?" It became clear to Bettina that people have a certain expectation of her because of her role. Fair or unfair, they expect more patience, warmth, and empathy from her than from the other directors. In her zeal to get things done, Bettina wasn't taking the time to show people that side of her personality.*

People's expectations of you will vary depending on the context. Part of your pre-sense is knowing what others expect of you in that context so that you can deliver.

Listening to Build Bridges, Not Walls

The listening skill for the left circle is "listening to build bridges." Imagine you and I are standing on opposite sides of a river, and we want to speak together, face to face. I could plunk myself down on my side and wait for you to build a bridge to me, or you could plunk yourself down on your side and wait for me to come to you. Either way, we have a long wait. Suppose we could figure out a way to build from both sides at once and end up (miraculously) at the same spot in the middle? Now that would save time and effort (and it would feel more "fair" to us, wouldn't it?).

When we listen to build bridges, we are listening for the opportunity to end up in the same place. Yes, we know all about our side of the river, otherwise known as our point of view, but leaders who listen begin with the belief that "they" have a point of view too, and the riverbank is equally lovely and special on "their" side. Stephen Covey says, "Seek first to understand, then to be understood." With that in mind, consider the story of Robert.

> Robert is a new VP and supply chain manager for a mid-sized manufacturing company. He was brought in to find cost-savings opportunities, including streamlining the number of vendors the company worked with and identifying those vendors who provided the highest quality service for the most reasonable price. Robert attacked his new role with speed and vigor. He wrote new rules, set new standards, and trimmed the

vendor list by 65 percent. He then held a series of meetings to inform and educate the various business heads regarding the new requirements. At one of the meetings, another long-service VP (and head of one of the company's flagship products) interrupted Robert in the middle of his presentation to state, flat out, that he had a long relationship with one of the vendors who was removed from the preferred provider list and he was going to continue to work with that vendor "no matter what." Robert was stunned at first, and then he engaged in an argument with the VP, defending his position against what he perceived to be a public challenge and loudly stating and restating the rules. Each party dug in and the argument escalated until the others felt uncomfortable and embarrassed and left one by one.

The next day Robert's boss called him in to discuss what happened, and once again things started to escalate. Robert's boss was unhappy and embarrassed by the quickly spreading tales from the previous day's debacle, so his patience was a little thin. In what felt like yet another attack on his ability to do his job, Robert immediately became defensive again. "That jerk was unbelievable!" he said loudly. "I was just doing the job you asked me to do. He acts as if the rules don't apply to him. You can fire me if you want, but I know I was right."

There's a lot going on here. First, what do you see as the provocative data points in this scenario?

_____

_____

_____

Here's what jumped out to me:

1. The long-service VP who, in an aggressive manner himself, interrupted Robert's presentation to challenge the new policy (displaying rude and uncivil conduct)

2. Robert's behavior in the meeting as he reacted instead of responding (he got triggered emotionally and was also uncivil)

3. Robert's defensive behavior with his boss when he allowed himself to get emotional again

4. Robert's insistence that, because *he was right*, his emotional and aggressive behavior was justified

Remember what we said about triggers and personal values in Chapter Three? What is triggering Robert emotionally, besides being interrupted? Think about what that emotion is attached to: what do you think is Robert's most deeply held value?

_____

_____

_____

_____

I'll bet you guessed it: Robert has a powerful need to be right. In fact, I often say being right is one of the worst things that can happen to your presence. Why is that, do you think?

_____

_____

_____

You know why from your own experience: an overzealous belief that we are right causes us to dig in, and what shows up is stubbornness, lack of listening, and a fair amount of self-righteousness. The impact of all of that "being right" on someone's presence is really negative. Not only is it a turn-off to the other people in the conversation, but being right can cause us to blindly defend our position, often vehemently, rather than trying to listen to the other person and create an open dialog. It causes a sort of temporary blindness and deafness. If I am suddenly blind, deaf, *and* emotionally challenged, how present am I? Right. I'm not.

Still, you might find a little part of yourself agreeing with Robert, at least in principle. After all, he was provoked by the rude behavior of the other VP when he was only trying to do his job. But remember what we said way back in Chapter One: *demonstrating executive presence is your job too.* Now, suppose Robert had responded with a question instead of a statement? Suppose Robert had said something like this: "Tell me more about your vendor. What makes them a desirable partner in your eyes?" and then had listened patiently and openly to the VP's answer. What might have changed in that meeting, and why?

_____

_____

_____

See the possibilities now? All kinds of good things could have happened:

➲ Robert might have learned more about the needs of the product group; perhaps there was something his team overlooked in their zeal to get the job done.

➲ The other VP would have felt heard. It is possible that he was grandstanding because he hadn't felt heard before.

➲ Robert could have asked a few more questions to learn more about the VP's situation, and in turn he could have offered some additional insight to the VP with the goal of building a bridge instead of a wall.

➲ Everyone could have stayed in the room and participated in the discussion, and Robert could have built some valuable social capital by his deft handling of the gruff VP.

There is significant upside for Robert to work on his presence and to examine what shows up when he feels attacked. If you were his boss (and you were in a calm state of mind), how would you coach Robert?

_____

_____

_____

_____

Oh, and by the way, we could spend a few pages talking about what the gruff VP should or shouldn't have done, but he wasn't my client. Robert was my client, and Robert needed to learn how to bring his best self into the room and keep it there, even when challenged by someone like that. Here's how I coached him:

➲ We started by focusing on his triggers and hot buttons, as described in Chapter One, so Robert could spot his early warning signs and get ahead of the hijack. I pointed out several examples of Robert's need to be right that showed up in our sessions. He admitted that he always felt put down personally when someone disagreed with him[18] and when it was done publicly, it instantly made him feel defensive and angry. Together we practiced the long, slow, deep breaths needed to slow the heart rate and avoid his emotional red zone.

⮑ One of Robert's strengths in supply chain management is his ability to weigh many different options. We brainstormed a list of open-ended questions that Robert could use in the meetings to allow people to voice their ideas, suggestions, and even objections.

- If Robert's goal for that meeting was to make a decision, he could choose the best option and explain his reasoning to the group.

- If his goal for the meeting was to build buy-in through consensus, he could acknowledge all of the ideas that surfaced, ensuring everyone felt heard, and vet a possible solution in the room.

⮑ Finally, Robert needs to write a rule for himself regarding temper tantrums at work. He would not allow his five-year-old to display that kind of behavior in a public place, so he needs to have a zero tolerance policy for himself— before the company does it for him.

Presence is ultimately about being other-conscious. The secret to making the Leaders with Presence list is to consistently and genuinely make it about "them."

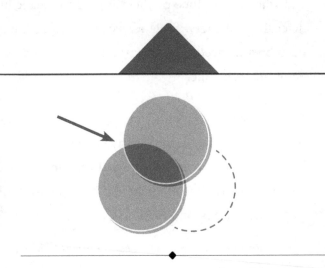

In our presence model, the overlap between the top and left circles is devoted to "Sensitive to style and cultural differences." For example, instruments like the Myers-Briggs Type Inventory® help one to be more informed and in tune with one's own style preferences, and to accept the fact that other people have different but acceptable style preferences. To connect, we must adapt accordingly. In our global economy, awareness of differences between country cultures is essential. There are excellent books and articles that are worth pursuing so you can be situationally aware.

MOMENT TO
REFLECT

◆

- ❏ Presence is only presence if you are with other people either virtually or in person; what matters is what one does, not what one would have done.

- ❏ For important interactions, be clear on your purpose and plan your approach in advance.

- ❏ For rapport to grow, the proper conditions need to exist.

- ❏ People will trust each other when there is credibility, transparency, rapport, and a common focus.

- ❏ What others expect of you will vary depending on the context you are in, and we move between contexts often in the course of the work day.

◆

5

COMMUNICATION IS PRESENCE IN ACTION

Kyle is a very tall man. He was nearly six feet tall in the eighth grade, a foot above the other students in his class. He developed the habit of slouching early on when he walked down the hall and when sitting in a group. Many years later, in the corporate setting, Kyle is a respected financial analyst in a fairly high position. He is frequently called in to high-level meetings to offer an opinion on trends in the market. He delivers cogent, succinct narratives, but sits hunched over in his seat, eyes down on his paper.

◆

Jenna is a well-regarded paralegal working inside a prestigious publishing company. She attends law school at night and is earning excellent grades. She hopes her current employer will consider her for a staff attorney position when she graduates and passes the bar. Jenna has come a long way from her humble beginnings, though she retains the strong "blue collar" accent of her Bronx childhood.

◆

Avery is a mid-level manager who is respected for his achievements and well liked for his warm, outgoing personality. When Avery was promoted to be the head of the unit, his people were genuinely happy for him and for themselves. Although they enjoy his garrulous style, he can ramble a bit, so they sometimes leave staff meetings confused about the overall direction or what they are supposed to do next.

◆

What do you notice about the three leaders described above?

_____

_____

_____

You probably noticed that

➲ they are all successful;

➲ they are all knowledgeable;

- ➲ they all lack awareness about an important element of their communication; and so

- ➲ they are not managing a critical component of their presence.

PREMISE #8

All Communication Is Your Presence in Action

Think about it: once you become a manager or team leader, there are very few times in the day when you are not communicating. Perhaps you're responding to an e-mail. Perhaps you're listening to your team member explain their idea. Perhaps you're leaving a voicemail message for your boss. Our days are full of communication, and so we are going to devote quite a bit of time and space to the part of the presence model which focuses on those aspects of communication that impact, and are impacted by, your presence. While we spend a good amount of time talking about presentation effectiveness in this chapter, you'll also notice that we share many examples and techniques that have nothing to do with formal presentations. Opportunities to communicate and demonstrate presence are 24/7, and like Marvin from Chapter Two, we want you to manage your communication moments all the time, not just when you are in the spotlight. Because there is so much material to share regarding communication and brand, we've split this content into two parts:

Part 1: Communication, to be covered in Chapter Five

Part 2: Brand, to be covered in Chapter Six

Heads Up's Presence Model: Communication and Brand

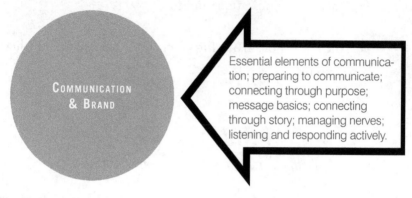

COMMUNICATION
& BRAND

Essential elements of communication; preparing to communicate; connecting through purpose; message basics; connecting through story; managing nerves; listening and responding actively.

PART 1:
COMMUNICATION

- Essential elements of communication

- Preparing to communicate

- Connecting through purpose

- Message basics

- Connecting through story

- Managing nerves

- Listening and responding actively

Essential Elements of Communication:
Look, Sound, and Content

Every time you communicate—speak, listen, or write—you create one or more visible or audible data points that impact presence. Some of these are created consciously in order to achieve your purpose, while others are created unconsciously due to a lack of awareness. Regardless of your intent, remember that people will connect the data points in a pattern that makes sense to them and from which they will draw conclusions that become "the truth" about you from their own points of view. So, we have to pay attention to all the ways that we communicate, not just our words.

Take another look at the three leaders' stories at the beginning of this chapter and answer these questions:

1.   In each case, which data point most needs to be managed?

Kyle: _____

Jenna: _____

Avery: _____

2.   What is the risk to each leader if he or she does not manage that element?

Kyle: _____

Jenna: _____

Avery: _____

Let's see how you did:

1. Kyle needs to manage his posture, an element of the way he **looks**. Jenna needs to manage her accent, an element of the way she **sounds**. Avery needs to organize the way he expresses his ideas, an element of his **content**.

2. The risk that Kyle faces is that when he slumps and looks down, he may appear less than confident when speaking to the executive team, which means they may wonder if they can really trust what he is saying. Jenna risks sounding far less educated than she really is and her employers might wonder if she is intelligent enough for a staff attorney position. The risk with Avery is that the people above him will see him as "more sizzle than steak," while his team may lose patience with his hazy communication and tune out, or worse, execute a task incorrectly because they did not understand his message.

In all three situations we have a very talented person whose potential is being obfuscated by an overlooked or mismanaged element of communication, and in every case when the issue was brought to their attention, their first response was basically, "What? This little issue? Do people really read that much into it?"

Yes, they do.

Remember from Chapter 2:

All communication is a combination of three things:

➲ How you look

➲ How you sound

➲ The content of your message

We must manage these "essential elements" to support our purpose. If the message is mixed, people pay much more attention to what they see and how it sounds than to the actual text or words.

We've already introduced you to some of the essential elements of look, sound, and content in this book, especially in the three stories at the start of this chapter. There are many more. By now you are no doubt wondering: "How am *I* doing? Do *I* have any of these developmental opportunities? What are *my* strengths to build on?" In the spirit of "know thyself" take a look at this detailed list of essential elements and see if you can determine which ones contribute to or detract from your presence.

ESSENTIAL ELEMENTS
CHECKLIST

Elements of Look

❑ Eye contact: Equates with confidence. The goal is to make sustained eye contact at key moments such as when shaking hands. When presenting, strive for sustained eye contact with each person in the room, no matter how big the audience. Avoid fleeting glances, looking up to think, or reading from your notes. Eye contact takes practice for more introverted people. In video conferences, be sure to make eye contact by looking directly into the camera, especially at the start and the end of a sentence.

❑ Facial expression: Appropriate use of smile, brow lift, or frown; avoid being overly animated or reserved; emotions need to be evident without being distracting. Pay attention to your "listening face" when not presenting, especially in a video conference. Ensure you are lighted properly so that your facial expressions can be seen. Note: Facial expressions show up *in your voice* when on the phone.

❑ Shoulders, hands, and arms: Shoulders should be dropped/relaxed versus hunched/tense; hand gestures reinforce key messages; arms loose at the sides when standing. In a videoconference, hand gestures should be used visibly from time to time when speaking, and your head and shoulders should be clearly in the frame.

❑ Posture: Equates with confidence. The goal is to sit or stand straight without being stiff. When standing, head and shoulders should be aligned over hips and feet. If speaking while seated, either in a meeting room or on a video call, do not lean on the table (cuts off the breath and stunts gestures.) Instead, support your core by using "seat in the chair and feet on the floor" position, like a tripod. On a video call, position the camera so that you can sit up straight.

❏ Unconscious or habitual movements: Anything distracting like pen clicking, finger tapping, foot or leg jiggle, swiveling in the chair, swaying or "box step" when standing creates a *second story* (See box on page 149.)

❏ Clothing, makeup, jewelry: Should enhance not distract. Too much makeup or jewelry is distracting; avoid overt perfume or aftershave; clothing must be good quality and very good fit. Check shoes and socks/stockings for wear. When working remotely, take care that shirts/tops are professional looking and appropriate for each videoconference.

❏ Handouts, slides, reports: All are a component of "Look" and must be aligned with the purpose and image of the speaker/writer. Slides that are messy, wordy, and unreadable have the same unconscious impact as wearing your pajamas to the office.

Elements of Sound

❏ Speed of speech: Too fast or too slow will cause the audience to disengage; rushing through a presentation suggests the low confidence of a junior person. The pace needs to slow down on technical phrases, large numbers, quotes; variations in speed engage listeners and support key messages, especially on conference calls.

❏ Use of pauses: Full pauses at ends of sentences allow time to breathe and think ahead. Pause before/after key words and important numbers so listeners can grasp the importance. Speech can sound rushed when pauses are clipped. Use longer pauses to await answers during Q&A.

❑ Volume: Too loud or soft will annoy audience; variations in volume support key messages and engage listeners. Set volume considering size of room, audience, and presence of sound-deadening items like carpeting, fans, street noise, etc.

❑ Tonality (melody or monotone): Melody is engaging and supports the key messages. Use the "Key Word Lift" to engage listeners by raising the pitch and volume slightly when speaking important words in a sentence. Avoid rising pitch at the ends of sentences ("scoop"); melody springs from speaker's real emotions about a topic. Avoid trap of atonal speech (flat melody) when communicating virtually and remember that some PC or camera mics deaden vocal tone.

❑ Pronunciation: Strive for crisp and audible pronunciation of all words, especially word endings.

❑ Filler (umm, uhhh, you know, "like," etc.): Creates subtext of lack of confidence; can create a "second story." Usually appears when speaker is rushing or underprepared and is often unconscious and habitual. The remedy for filler is the studied breath. See page 191.

❑ Accent: Regional accents can be associated with stereotypes; strong country-of-origin accents make it harder for audience to understand. The goal is clarity. Accent reduction specialists can help speakers improve pronunciation.

Elements of Content

- ❑ Organization/Flow: Content follows logical sequence; clear beginning, middle and end.

- ❑ Focus/Brevity: Appropriate amount of detail for time available and audience needs; key messages brief and memorable. Overtalking suggests the speaker is underprepared or lacks maturity or confidence.

- ❑ Clarity of Purpose: Speaker is clear on desired impact (what the listener should feel, think, or do) and purpose goes beyond the simple goal of "to inform."

- ❑ Key messages apparent: Clearly communicates what, how, and why in every message.

- ❑ Point of view (POV): Has an informed point of view; can articulate own opinion/POV when asked.

- ❑ Run-on speech: Overuse of "and" or "so" between phrases creates long run-on sentences that are hard to follow. Can be a form of filler. Beware of tangents that cause speaker and audience to lose the thread.

- ❑ Relevant to audience: Ideally, content reflects the audience's needs, interest,s and level.

- ❑ Jargon: With homogenous groups, jargon can be a connector. With mixed groups, it can be a barrier.

A Word About Virtual Meetings and the Essential Elements:

We rely more and more on conference calls and videoconferencing to come together from different locations. Conference calls are convenient but can be dreadfully boring and uninspiring. Whether you are on the phone or using video chat with cameras off, without the benefit of "look" all of your expressiveness and emotion has to come through "sound" and "content." Help people stay present and engaged:

- Do vary your vocal melody, pace, and volume to keep people engaged. Speak naturally, and ensure that everyone can hear you.

- Do make eye contact with the people in the conference room even when you are speaking to someone on the phone. It shows up in the voice.

- When it's your meeting, do let people know in advance that participation is welcome.

- Do use your mute button if there is distracting background noise in your workspace.

- Do remember to unmute yourself when you're ready to participate.

- Do use open-ended questions to encourage interaction, and pause long enough for people to be able to answer. Let some of the content come from them.

- Do not lean forward on the table and talk "at" the phone; it cuts off the air supply to your voice and flattens out your melody.

- Do not multitask. It shows in your voice and mannerisms, and you are missing opportunities to add value and demonstrate commitment.

- Do not assume that all virtual meetings have to be boring and mundane. When it's your meeting to run, you can make your own choices to increase engagement. Plan in advance.

That's quite a list, isn't it? But now what? Everything on the checklist impacts your presence and the ability of your audience to connect with you and your message, but you can't think about all those things while you're trying to have a conversation or present information at a meeting. What to do?

The fact is, you already do many of these things well, and so you don't need to think about those strengths at all. Focus on a few things … one bite at a time. Start by simply reviewing the list of essential elements and ask yourself which of these elements are strengths for you, or areas where you feel quite competent. Are there other elements that you suspect need work? And perhaps most importantly, how do you know, or how can you find out, if your assessment is correct?

_____

_____

_____

If you said you can find out from "feedback," you are correct.

- ➲ You can get constructive feedback from bosses, colleagues, or friends at work. Ask them to pay attention to something specific that you are working on, and then seek them out after the meeting for the feedback. Example: "Kelly, I've been working hard to be more succinct when I answer questions at meetings. Since you'll be at the staff meeting today, would you please listen to me and give me feedback after the meeting as to whether or not I rambled or went off on tangents?"

- ➲ If you present at town hall meetings or other big events that are video-recorded, you can request a copy and critique yourself, watching and listening for the essential elements. In addition, some videoconferences are recorded. Check with your company to see if you can access those for your own use and continued learning.

- ➲ Try to notice other people who are especially effective at an element you'd like to strengthen. Notice in detail what sets them apart, and then practice doing the same things yourself to the extent that it makes sense.

The "Second Story"

A "second story" is an interesting story that plays in the listener's head when the speaker does something so distracting that people's attention is on that rather than on the speaker's "first story." The distraction might be filler, unconscious repetitive movement, or even an unfortunate clothing choice.

If you ever sat in a class or meeting and counted the number of times the speaker said "uh" or "okay?" and even made those little hash marks on your notepad, then you have experienced the fun distraction of the second story.

Of course, no speaker wants to take attention away from their first story, which is why self-awareness and feedback are so important. Eliminate second stories by ensuring all of the essential elements are aligned with your message, and nothing is detracting from that. Ask a trusted colleague to watch your practice session, or video-record your own practice and critique yourself.

While we don't teach the remedies for all of the essential elements in this book, knowing what you want to work on makes it possible for you to seek help from any number of resources, including your own colleagues and friends.

Lastly, while the essential elements are seemingly "little things," they have a big impact on how you are perceived because they distract people from your real message. For more information on why it is important to eliminate distractions, see "Second Stories" box above.

Leaders who seek to be understood will manage all of the elements of look, sound, and content when presenting, conversing, and even when writing e-mails or texts. They prepare to ensure alignment and practice to increase confidence.

A Word about Video Conferences and the Essential Elements:

We rely more and more on video conferences to come together from different locations when air travel is not feasible. Video conferences are convenient but can be dreadfully boring and uninspiring. Without the benefit of "look," all of your expressiveness and emotion has to come through "sound" and "content." Help people stay present and engaged:

⮩ Do vary your vocal melody, pace, and volume to keep people engaged. Speak naturally, and ensure that everyone can hear you.

⮩ Do make eye contact with the people in the room even when you are speaking to someone on the phone. It shows up in the voice.

⮩ Do let people know in advance that participation is welcome.

⮩ Do use open-ended questions to encourage interaction, and pause long enough for people to be able to answer. Let some of the content come from them.

⮩ Do not lean forward on the table and talk at the phone; it cuts off the air supply to your voice and flattens out your melody.

⮩ Do not multitask when you are alone someplace, participating in the call. Not only does it show in your voice but you are missing opportunities to add value and demonstrate commitment.

⮩ Do not assume that all conference calls have to be boring and mundane. When it's *your* call to run, *you* can make your own choices to increase engagement.

Preparing to Communicate

After all my talk about being other-conscious, you might be surprised by my next statement: When it comes to preparation, *be selfish*. Here's why I say that. Does this story sound familiar?

> *Daryl knows he has to present the quarterly report at tomorrow's senior staff meeting. After all, he's usually the one who presents the report the one or two times a year when his boss is away. He hasn't thought much about it—too busy—although he's not worried about the content per se since he prepared 90 percent of the material that went into the report. All he needs is a half-hour to refresh himself on the document and anticipate any questions. Maybe he'll do that this morning, except that the phone rang off the hook and someone put a meeting on his calendar and, well, the morning got away from him. Maybe this afternoon ... oops, a little crisis and some critical e-mails needed his attention, plus that new person had a few questions and then it was after 6:00 PM. Finally, after helping his kids with their homework, he takes ten minutes to scan the report before falling asleep, convincing himself that's probably all the prep he needs.*

◆

Really? I don't think so.

But why does Daryl think so? I work with dozens of "Daryls" a year. They all tell me the same things:

- 💬 I already know this material,

- 💬 The senior staff members already know me,

- I just don't have time,

- Not much usually happens at these meetings anyway.

We call this "the trap of the simple assignment." Because it is routine, we kid ourselves into thinking we don't need to prepare. That's the trap.

1. Daryl may know the contents of the report, but he has spent no time thinking about what aspects of the report are most meaningful to the audience and thus should be highlighted, nor has he anticipated their questions and prepared cogent, informed answers in advance. He has fallen into the *trap of the simple assignment.* "I know this stuff, so I don't really need to prepare."

2. The senior staff members "know him," but how do they know him? Unless they have other data points than these occasional meetings, they likely see him as the reliable stand-in for his boss. Nothing more, nothing special, nothing unique, a good "placeholder" until the real guy gets back. And why? Because that is exactly what Daryl shows them every time.

3. There's "having the time" and there's "taking the time." Time is fungible. Most of my "Daryls" can manage to find forty-five minutes when other people make unexpected demands, but they don't or won't even give themselves fifteen minutes to think about their next interaction and make some decisions about the impact they want to have.

4. "Not much happens" at these meetings, and why? Ultimately it's because Daryl has trained his audience not to engage (or they've trained him) and therefore it's simply a transaction, not a conversation.

These are lost opportunities. Every time you communicate with others it is your presence in action. Every interaction is a data point. If all of Daryl's interactions are as unremarkable as his senior staff presentations, he will likely be rated in the middle of the performance-review rating scale, even though he will probably see himself as above average. He thinks that because he is the go-to guy for his boss, he is more of a star than his colleagues, but unless he shines a little more brightly, he's going to be overlooked at promotion or recognition time.

If you know someone—or you are—like Daryl, you need to put your own needs first when it comes to preparation, especially when the topic is something rather routine. Think of it like this: you know that announcement they make on airplanes about the cabin losing pressure and the oxygen masks dropping down? Remember what they tell you to do if you are traveling with a small child? Right. Put your own mask on first, and then assist your child. They tell us this over and over because it is every parent's gut instinct to try to save their child first, but while doing so, the parent can pass out and be of no use to the child or themselves. In this situation the airline is actually telling the parent to *be selfish*, just for a split second, so he or she will be able to help others later.

That is what I'm saying to you. Be selfish, just for this moment, so you can be of service to others later:

➲ Let's start with the "be selfish" part of the equation: when you take that prep time, you give yourself the luxury of planning, thinking, and organizing. You can anticipate questions, prepare examples or back-up documentation, get your head in the right place, and bring your best self to the meeting. How much prep time do you need? It depends, but I promise you this: preparation is like any other routine or skill; it gets faster and easier with repetition.

➲ As for the "be of service to others" part of the equation, you'll notice in the prep steps on page 155 that most of your prep is about them. Good presenters focus on giving the people what they want and need. Whether you are presenting at a meeting, video conference, or through a memo, a few moments of prep will enhance the outcome— and your reputation—dramatically. Find the time.

Yes, other people need you and want you and will make demands on your time, and you will feel you have to put them first. In my corporate days I felt that way. At one point my staff jokingly made up a "Take a number" sign outside my office, like they do at the deli counter—I get it! There are huge demands on your time and few breaks in the action, and now with e-mail and text messaging any break is immediately filled with "catching up on a few e-mails." It is expected, it is insidious, and it is the "new normal," so it takes real commitment and some white-knuckle determination to set aside the time you need to prepare and to stick to it.

A Chicken-or-Egg Dilemma:

Do you procrastinate doing your prep because it is so inefficient that it's not worth the time? OR do you not leave yourself enough time to prepare and so you rush it and don't do a good job preparing?

In other words, if your prep was more efficient, would you make the time for it?

Good news: here's a way to streamline your preparation that I'll bet is different from what you are doing now. For example, when someone asks you to present at a meeting, do you sit down at your computer and start creating or editing your "deck" in PowerPoint? If you said "Of course!", you are actually starting at the end of the process and making much more work for yourself. Look at the steps below. They suggest that you do a little thinking and planning before you ever touch PowerPoint. This works because you are beginning at the beginning, and everything flows from there.

Six Communication "Prep Steps" for Better Planning and Best Results

1. Identify your audience. Who is the intended audience and what do they want from you? Why are you the chosen presenter or writer? What unique perspective can you bring to them? If you don't know the answers to these questions, find out. Ask the meeting organizer or your boss or anyone who would know. If you don't know what they want from you, it makes it really hard to give it to them, and because we worry about satisfying our audience, this knowledge helps us focus our efforts and avoid the trap of throwing everything into the deck that might be important.

2. Clarify your goal or purpose. What is the purpose of this communication? What do you want people to do or feel as a result of your talk? How do *you* feel about the topic? Are you prepared to share your point of view or feelings authentically? Do you have a clear call to action? If you don't know your purpose, you are unlikely to achieve it.

3. Create the connections. Do you expect or want interaction? What will you do to engage the listener? How about folks on the phone? How will you stay connected with your audience and keep them connected to you? Do you want a formal or informal tone? What choices can you make about your content, handouts, slides, and so forth, to support that? Remember, presence is about connecting, so be deliberate about the choices you make rather than defaulting to a wordy handout or slideshow.

4. Collect your content. Assemble any supporting documentation you need to understand your topic deeply, and then select and include *only* those content elements that are most important to them, not to you. Organize your content to ensure a logical flow, and trim to fit time and space constraints. Every time you edit, edit with your audience in mind. Strive for brevity and clarity; let them ask you for more detail if needed.

5. Prepare your slides and handouts. As a last step, open up the PowerPoint template and start creating slides. Again, most people treat this like a first step, but how can you start making slides when you haven't done the analysis in Steps 1-4 above? This is how we end up with bloated, wordy decks, full of slides we couldn't possibly have the time to cover. Keep in mind that you may need three different documents:

   • **Projection slides to be shown on the screen:** keep these minimal in number and design; use more graphics[19] and white space, fewer words. If you don't really need slides, don't use them. Keep the focus on you.

- **Speaker notes:** things that you see but no one else sees. Do not put your speaker notes up as the projection slides. It makes the audience wonder why they need to listen to you when they can read it for themselves.

- **Handouts:** can be as robust as needed to support your presentation. Use an index and dividers if lengthy; consider an executive summary or note-taking outline in the front of the handout to keep people engaged.

At this point I know it seems counterintuitive that doing three different documents will actually save you prep time, but think about it: If you've ever tried to cram your speaker notes onto a slide that also includes tons of detail, the amount of time you spend formatting that wordy, crowded slide can be put to better use, allowing for cleaner, more audience-centric documents and ease of delivery for you.

6. Practice, practice, practice. Please get over your self-consciousness, practice out loud, and record yourself using your smartphone. The message just sounds different in our heads. If you are short on time, practice everything once so you can time your delivery, and then practice just your opening and closing several more times. Practice the answers to your anticipatory questions (see page 173.) Always prepare so that you run slightly under your allotted time. Avoid the trap of having too much material and having to rush or skip things.

These prep steps were created to help people streamline and optimize their preparation for presentations; however, if you are preparing a written memo, the same basic thought process applies:

- Know your audience, know your goal, choose your tone, collect your raw material, and then start writing. For Step 6 substitute "proofread" for "practice."

Connecting through Purpose

We first mentioned being clear on your purpose and approach in Chapter Two. We also talked about having a purpose or goal in the communication prep steps on page 155, but what does that mean? Let's see.

Do you remember the story of *Alice in Wonderland?* At one point in her journey Alice comes to a crossroads and stops short, not knowing which way to go. Spying the Cheshire cat above in a tree, she asks him which road she should take. The cat says that it depends on where she is trying to get to. Alice says she doesn't know, and the cat replies with his famous grin, "Then any road will get you there."

Preparing a presentation or writing a significant memo without knowing your purpose is like setting out on a journey with no clear destination. You will certainly cover some ground, but you'll never know if you've arrived, and you won't know you've gone astray until it's too late.

The purpose is what you want people to do, think, or feel as a result of your communiqué.

Most of the time we assume the purpose of our memo or our staff meeting presentation is simply "to inform" or "to update" others. That's fine, although it's mundane and a bit boring, and people don't really know what to do with that information, nor do they know how to feel about it.

By way of contrast, have you ever delivered a presentation that was anything but mundane and people walked away enthused, engaged, and with a sense of purpose...*your* purpose? Did you have that "yeah!" feeling afterwards? And did you wonder how you could create that sort of outcome every time? Think back; you were probably very clear on what you wanted people to feel and how you were going to accomplish that in your presentation. Was your goal:

- ➲ To motivate or inspire

- ➲ To recognize, thank, or praise

- ➲ To engage, stimulate, or connect

- ➲ To reassure or calm

- ➲ To caution or warn

- ➲ Or something else?

Compare the list above with the purpose "to inform." Which is the weakest? You're right; the weakest is "to inform." Consider infusing your message with the emotion and energy that comes with a more active and engaging purpose. Your purpose can be "to inform *and* motivate" for example.

Think about a speaker at your company whose recent presentation had you really engaged, maybe even all fired up. What did the speaker do that caused you and others to engage in this way? What do you remember about the person's:

- Vocal melody

- Rate of speech

- Vocal volume

- Facial expressions

- Arms and hands

- Body position

- Word choices

- Personal stories

- Group participation

- Call to action

- Other?

_____

_____

_____

_____

Now the next time you are at a meeting, notice which speaker causes you to disengage or fade in and out. Try to notice what that speaker is specifically doing, or not doing, with the above-mentioned communication elements that is causing you to feel that way, and make some notes here:

_____

_____

_____

_____

How much did you notice? The more you can pay attention and objectively critique what effective speakers are doing, the more you'll train your own eyes and ears, making it easier to coach yourself as well as spot the opportunities for greatness in others.

Now here's the payoff question: Do you observe uninspiring presenters like the one you described earlier and think that this is okay because it's the norm? That this is the way it is supposed to be? If you said yes, that's a little depressing, but you are not alone. Sadly, we learn that droning, sing-song, report-out delivery style when we are corporate newbies, and we think, "Oh, okay, it's a little robotic, but if that's the way business presentations are supposed to sound, then so be it."

Not true! Why can't the norm be inspirational and energizing?

And how? By connecting to your purpose. Once you connect to your purpose, your own emotions will be activated. This in turn will allow your natural expressiveness to shine through, and people will connect to you and your ideas.

How Much Emotional Expression Is Enough?

And how much is too much? The answer depends on three things: your purpose, your audience, and your personal style. In the diagram on page 198 describing the overlap between self-management and communication, the behavior we are aiming for is "managing feelings so they are expressed appropriately." You may have strong feelings about something, for instance, and a full expression of those emotions might be very necessary with one audience and a terrible idea with a different audience. You always want to ask yourself: What is my purpose, what do they need from me, and what am I comfortable giving them in terms of emotion?

Deciding how much emotion to show is like having your hand on a dimmer switch when you're setting the mood in your dining room. Too high and you ruin the mood. Too low and you can't see the soup. The diagram below shows a range of emotional expression from low to high. The darkly shaded areas would be considered too low or too high, but the whole lighter center section is acceptable for communicating at work.

OUR EXPRESSION-O-METER

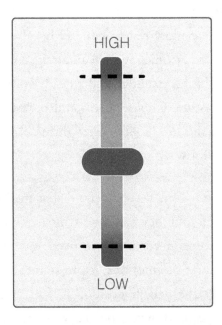

So where do *you* set the level? As we said, it depends on your purpose, your audience, and your natural style.

For example:

➲ If your purpose is "to inspire" and your audience is open and trusting, you would want to be higher on the meter than your usual delivery style. How high depends on your personal comfort level and style. For many Americans, the ideal range would be in the mid-to-high range of the meter. To accomplish this, you would use broader gestures and livelier facial expressions, and you should use more vocal variation in order to engage. Your word choices should be inspirational too. Choose words such as "vision," "achieve," "win," "succeed," "together," and so forth.

⊃   If your purpose is "to calm" and your audience is anxious, you should be just below the center of the meter. Gestures should be more restrained, and facial expressions should be serious at times and encouraging at other times. Good eye contact is essential, and a steady vocal pace will soothe and reassure. Choose words and phrases such as "careful consideration," "solid," "thoughtful," "plan," "confident," and so forth.

Sometimes people tell me they are afraid that their gestures are too big, or they've been told they flail their arms around too much when they present. Gestures need to be practiced and perfected just like content. The amount of emotional expression drives, and is driven by, your purpose. The default position is not zero. If you are too low on the expression-o-meter, people will tune out, disconnect, and maybe even fall asleep. If you are too high, they'll be turned off by "the drama" and won't take you seriously. Choose your purpose, choose your approach with deliberation, and then reinforce your purpose through thoughtful gestures and excellent content.

Mark Your Territory:

When feasible, practice in the space where your in-person presentation will be will be held. Try using various gestures and different levels of vocal volume while standing at the podium or walking around the room. If using a remote to advance your slides, practice using the remote. If you will be seated at a conference table, survey the room in advance and get a sense of the acoustics while seated.

Message Basics: How to Prepare Content Efficiently and Effectively

I'll never forget the day: I was sitting through yet another round of back-to-back presentations at our annual strategic planning offsite in the windowless ballroom of a local hotel along with 150 of my nearest and dearest colleagues, when I glanced at the agenda and saw that Albert was scheduled for the 4:30 PM timeslot. I groaned under my breath and whispered to my coworker, "Oh no, it's Albert. We are definitely not getting out of here by five." She rolled her eyes in mock agony. "Why would they put him last?" she whispered. It didn't make sense to me, either. Albert is a talker, and everyone knows he's a talker. And while he has really interesting things to say, he just has too many of them and goes into way too much detail on each one. I wished I could look forward to Albert's presentation, I really did. He's a nice guy and he's smart. But honestly, it had already been a really long day.

◆

There are Alberts everywhere who haven't yet grasped the concept that brevity is a good thing. Messages that are overly long, loaded with detail, and convoluted with tangents are ineffective and frustrating for the listener, and yet we all fall into the trap of trying to jam too much content into our time slot. If ever the phrase "less is more" is appropriate, it is in the creation of our presentation content.

You can be brief and still be complete. People overtalk when they aren't sure they've covered everything. Using the time-honored key message-headline model below, you can be sure you've hit the main points.

To be complete, every well-constructed business message includes these three content elements:

1. The what: the main concept or big idea that you are there to discuss

2. The how: the central action you are advocating or that was taken

3. The why: the outcome, result, or rationale; what I call the big "so what?"

Together, these three components are combined to form the key message of your presentation. The key message is a short statement or group of phrases that introduce the gist of your presentation. It is complete while also being brief.

The *what*, the main concept, is always expressed as a **noun**, while the *how*, the central action, is always expressed as a **verb**.

In a speech, the key message might sound like one of these examples:

"Today we're here to talk about the *plan* (what) to reorganize, how we will *implement* (how) the transition program, and the expected productivity *gains* (why)."

"And now, Sheila will talk about the *status* (what) of the Sunrise Project, the next steps *to be taken* (how), and the *benefits* (why) we expect once implemented."

"Our purpose then is to discuss the potential *staff reductions* (what), the *cost savings* (why) that will result, and the steps to *move forward* (how) with the action plan."

Notice we switched up the order in the third example to what-why-how. When the why is more important or urgent to your audience than the how, switch the order in your key message and carry that same order through your presentation. Audiences that are nervous or stressed by the topic may need to hear the rationale before they can listen to the next steps or action plan.

Beware: in business, the *what* is often an action that we are recommending or reporting on, and it makes it difficult at first to craft the key message. For instance, if my presentation is about something my team did, is that a *what* or is that a *how* in my message? I can't answer that here without knowing more about the real presentation, but some helpful examples are on the next page. On the right side, notice that the what, how, and why are underlined, and the last example is in the alternative what-why-how order.

Examples of the Key Message

Wrong	Right
I'm here to talk about changing the Q4 budget.	I'm here to talk about our <u>recommendation</u> for changes to the Q4 budget, how we <u>determined</u> those changes, and the expected <u>impact</u> on the bottom line.
Today we need to discuss realigning resources to handle the new business coming in.	Today we are going to discuss <u>resource requirements</u> and <u>analyze</u> what we have and what we need so that we can <u>successfully handle</u> the new business coming in.
Our goal for this meeting is to come up with ways of keeping the customer service people in compliance.	Our goal for this meeting is to create new <u>guidelines</u> that will help customer service personnel <u>stay in compliance and keep us open for business</u>. We'll also discuss how to <u>implement</u> the guidelines across the division.

Talk like an Egyptian

As you can see from all of these examples, the key message is really a short introduction that tells your listener what to expect from your presentation. Of course, you can't just stop there. Like the stone blocks that make up the great pyramids, the building blocks in our message structure depend on the items below them to make sense. As shown in the pyramid diagram on your right, the key message 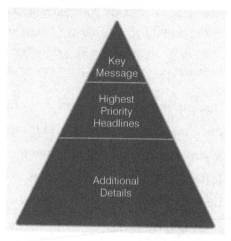 is supported by those "headlines," which are the most important ideas needed to flesh out the key message for this audience. In turn, those headlines are supported by additional details.

How big should this pyramid be? The overall size of the pyramid equates to the amount of content you will need in order to satisfy your audience *and* come in under the time allowed. Imagine that the size of this page is everything you could say about your topic, while the size of the pyramid is the amount of time you'll actually have. This means you have to leave out a lot of your favorite material, and leave in only that content that is of interest to *them*.

How many headlines are enough? How much detail is too much? Once again, it depends on

1. how much time you have, and

2. what is most important to the audience.

The more time you have, and the more detail they want, the larger the pyramid will be.

The tip of the pyramid never changes size, because the key message is always brief, clear and uncluttered. To state the key message, you likely need about thirty to sixty seconds. The bottom two sections of the pyramid will expand or contract depending on the length of time available for your presentation and the amount of detail your audience wants. The more time you have, the more headlines you can cover and/or the more detail you can share, as long as *all* of your content is selected based upon what the audience wants from you.

The hardest part of any presentation is deciding what to leave out. By the time we reach a certain level, we know so much and we can talk for hours about our area of expertise, especially with people from our field or function. But that's not what *they* want; the folks in our audience are only interested in the slice of our expertise that is relevant to them. So you need to think like Michelangelo, who believed that the statue "was already living inside the block of marble," and all he had to do was carve awayanything that did not belong. "I saw the angel in the marble and carved until I set him free." It was not by adding more that he made it perfect; it was by taking away the excess.

Putting the Model to Work

Have you ever heard of this old guideline for making presentations?

⊃   Tell 'em what you're going to tell 'em,

⊃   Tell 'em, then

⊃   Tell 'em what you told 'em.

There's actually a kernel of wisdom in that. It says you need to prepare people to listen, and then deliver your content, and then summarize at the end to help cement the ideas into people's heads. Using the same principle in the box on page 171, notice how we nestle the key message and headlines in a "wrapper" that positions our message perfectly between an engaging opening and closing:

KMH and the Flow of Your Presentation

1. Begin with opening remarks, welcome, and perhaps an opening anecdote. This is called "The Wrapper."

2. State the **Key Message** as one uninterrupted thought to introduce your subject.

3. Transition to the main concept (WHAT) and deliver all of your highest priority "WHAT" **headlines** with supporting **details**, starting with the headlines that are most important to the audience. (Note: if pressed for time, trim from the bottom of each headline list, i.e., the *lowest* priority for audience, and also trim detail.)

4. Transition to the main actions taken or proposed (HOW) and deliver the highest priority **headlines** with supporting **details** as above, most important headlines first. Each HOW headline should start with a verb to connote action.

5. Transition to the **headlines** spelling out the benefits/ outcomes achieved or expected (WHY) as a result of the action starting with the highest priority headlines and supporting **details**.

6. Summarize by restating the **Key Message**, perhaps paraphrasing slightly for emphasis.

7. End with a closing anecdote, call to action, or Q&A.

8. Say "Thank you."

You now have an overview of *what* the key message-headline (KMH) approach is, *how* it supports the flow of your content, and the *benefits* it brings to you and your audience. (See the what, how, and why in that sentence? This structure appears in many places throughout this book!) This basic structure ensures your message is complete and addresses the main things that people want to know. It works for formal or informal presentations, short updates, and when communicating in person, on the phone, or in writing.[20] When we teach this method to individuals and groups around the world, the simplicity of the KMH model really resonates. It helps you keep your content focused and well organized, which streamlines both your preparation and your delivery.

Beware of a common trap in business communication. In my experience, most everyday presentations and memos usually do a good job of communicating the main idea (what) and the actions that will follow (how) but not a very good job of explaining the why—namely, the rationale behind the main idea. That's too bad, because that's where all of the energy and emotion live.

Why do folks leave out the best part? Perhaps they think their audience already knows the reason, so no need to explain. Perhaps they fear that if they talk about the rationale it opens it up for criticism. However, in my experience, most presenters leave out the why because they don't really know the compelling rationale behind the what. The message was cascaded down to them and the why got lost somewhere along the way. Here's the thing: there's a compelling why out there someplace. If we operate under the assumption that decisions are made in organizations for good reasons, we need to find out that original good reason. Then we can communicate the decision authentically.

> A technique called "the Five Whys" is useful when retracing a decision to get back to the original reason why a change has been made or a process reworked. Coming out of process engineering, it is a method of uncovering the root cause of a problem or situation without attacking or blaming. There's a wealth of information about this technique on the Internet. Start with Wikipedia under "the Five Whys." For an example of decisions gone awry, look up the Abilene paradox.

Two more KMH tips: (1) When you spend a few moments thinking about your audience and your purpose as advised in the Six Prep Steps starting on page 155, you will find it faster and easier to choose which headlines to leave in and which ones to take out because you'll approach your preparation based on the audience's needs instead of your own. (2) As you create your content in the KMH format, and you're making decisions based on the audiences needs and wants, at some point you'll likely say to yourself, "Hmm ... I think people will have questions about this." Whenever you think of a question that the audience might have, write it down. Keep a separate sheet of paper near you for what we call **"anticipatory questions"** and write down every question you think your audience will ask or might ask. Then, prepare your answers and practice them when you practice your presentation. You can provide that information when asked during the Q&A, or you can build it into your presentation if you think the majority of people in the audience are interested in that item. We strongly suggest that you also write down any questions that you hope they won't ask, and figure out in advance how you want to handle it if it comes up at the presentation. Preparing your anticipatory questions in advance will decrease your nervousness and help you demonstrate presence and poise. Moreover, practicing them and then putting them on the back burner in your head allows you to focus on your prepared remarks, and gets you out of your head and into the room so you can be fully present with your audience.

The Surprise around the Corner

Has this ever happened to you? It's first thing in the morning and you're walking into your building when someone stops you in the hallway and asks you a question about something that happened last week, or last month, or even yesterday. And there you stand, struggling to compose your thoughts so you can present them in a brief, well-organized way, all the while trying to carry your coffee, your briefcase, your coat, and maybe keep walking without bumping into anything. Not easy, huh?

Suppose you had a magical formula that would help you organize your response in a snap so you appear poised, prepared, and present all the time? Of course you would. Before you say "abracadabra" let me share a story:

> Delia is an experienced contracts specialist working for a financial services company. She has been with the firm for a long time and has an amazing memory regarding complex deals the company has brokered over the years. She is seen as a valuable resource and is the go-to person for many of the younger contract analysts. Over the years, others in Delia's peer group have all been promoted to senior VP while Delia has remained a VP despite her boss's best efforts to get a promotion approved by the CEO.

> When pressed for the reason behind his decision, the CEO provided the following observations:

- *She gets completely tongue tied whenever he asks her a question in the hallway or elevator.*

- *Her office is a "disaster area" with papers everywhere.*

- *Her clothing, while expensive, is ill fitting (too big) and looks rumpled and disheveled.*

"In summary," the CEO said, "she's disorganized and self-conscious. Frankly, I am underwhelmed."

◆

This is understandable when you look at the data points, especially the first one. The CEO is asking Delia about deals that she is intimately involved in. He expects her to know the answers. But Delia gets so nervous around the CEO that she stumbles and uses lots of filler ("um," "uh") while she tries to figure out how to phrase the answer. If you were the CEO, would you feel comfortable bringing Delia in to the board room to present a major new deal? That's what SVPs have to do. Everyone else who works with Delia cannot believe that someone with her technical knowledge and experience has not yet been promoted. Their data points are different. Delia is comfortable with them and has no trouble answering any and all questions. This is the argument Delia's boss makes when he lobbies for her promotion, only to receive the feedback mentioned above.

We understand feeling tongue-tied when surprised, and we'll talk about that in a moment. The other two issues are legitimate and seem within Delia's control: why didn't she dress better and clean up her office? When I asked her, she gave many of the same reasons that other dedicated, busy working professionals give me: who has time? Is this really a priority? She was a little defensive about her clothing, although she did admit that she did not know how to shop for clothes that would flatter her body type and would simply buy whatever outfit was on the mannequin. She was also a little defensive about the piles in her office. "It might look disorganized to you, but I know where everything is, and I can put my finger on anything I'm looking for!" Hmm … not much motivation to spend a couple of weeks "organizing" the paper piles, is there?

Delia's situation is a perfect example of the importance of managing one's executive presence 24/7. These data points have nothing to do with formal presentations or matters of substance. These data points are everyday occurrences that form a pattern which incorrectly labels a talented professional, preventing her from fully contributing at work.

All is not lost, however. First of all, while the CEO has a strong point of view about Delia, he is known as an open-minded guy. Second, Delia has a solid technical reputation to build upon. Third, her boss is not ready to give up on this promotion. Finally, as we've learned, data points can be managed.

If you were Delia's boss or one of her good friends, what advice would you give her?

_____

_____

_____

_____

You probably started with the big obvious things that are more easily managed with the right support: she could work with a personal shopper and get a good tailor to polish her appearance. She could enlist a temp or even hire a professional organizer to help straighten out her office. Good start, because right now these seemingly insignificant elements of appearance are masking her other contributions. Delia was open to working with a personal shopper, although she still resisted the notion of "cleaning" her office. "Okay," I thought at the time, "One bite at a time."

My favorite part of my work with Delia was to help her prepare for those unexpected conversations. The CEO's most frequent exposure to Delia came in the elevator or in the common areas. Delia got flustered when he asked her a question, not because she didn't know the answer but because she didn't know how to answer the question in a crisp, concise manner. She said she became flustered and stumbled through a half-answer because she felt surprised. "You can't possibly know who you're going to run into, right?" she asked.

Wrong.

You absolutely can anticipate with a reasonable degree of certainty who you will run into and what they might ask you, and you can prepare an answer to a supposedly unexpected question in advance.

When I started working as Delia's coach, I asked her, "When you run into the CEO or one of the other executives, what kinds of questions do they ask you?"

"Well," she replied, "They usually ask me about one of the deals we are working on, or what happened in the meeting with the lawyers, that sort of thing. If it's the CFO, she likes a little more detail around the numbers, and I know the numbers inside and out, but I just can't seem to come up with the answer I want in that moment."

This is great information. She actually has a pretty good idea of what they are going to ask her because it usually concerns a current project or deal she is working on. She even knows who likes to receive their answer in a certain way.

You can, too. The first step in preparing any answer is to anticipate the asker's question. Let's start with some typical hallway or elevator questions. They probably sound like these:

"I'm glad I ran into you ...

1. I have a meeting with my boss later this morning. Where are we on the Applewood project?"

2. I heard there was a serious customer complaint yesterday. What's going on there?"

3. I couldn't make the sales meeting. What happened on the Doolittle account?

4. The report deadline has shifted. What can you get me by 3:00 PM today?

Sound familiar? Anyone who has worked in an organization has been stopped en route with a question like this. So it's not entirely unexpected, right? You just need to do a little prep work. Think about what you are working on now, and then think about whom you might run into and what they might ask you. When I do this activity in my seminars, it takes a few minutes of thought, and then people come up with several questions depending on what they are working on or who they will see in the next few days.

Next, you need to have your answer ready. We recommend the SAR(s) model below. This model and others like it have been around for a very long time because they are a simple and effective way to organize your thoughts and respond to hallway questions.

The SAR(s) Model

Situation/status: *Provides a brief overview of the situation at hand or provides a bit of context for the questioner. Be brief, no more than three sentences, just enough information so the listener can take in the rest of your answer, which is what the questioner really wants to know.*

Actions taken or planned: *Objectively describes the relevant steps taken or planned, with enough detail to answer the underlying, unspoken question "What is being done about this?"*

Result/response expected: *Outlines the effect that the actions had or will have on the problem, situation, relationship, and so forth.*

(Support needed, if any): *This is in parentheses because it is optional. You don't always need support from the person asking the question, but if you do, now is the time to ask for it.*

Example:

"Hey, Chuck, I'm glad I caught you. What happened with the Hollister customer complaint yesterday?"

Situation: "Well, as you probably heard, the shipment was two weeks late for the second month in a row, and Carmen was furious."

Action: "So Miranda drove out to Fairville to speak with Carmen and hand-deliver the shipment, and I stayed here to review the process and figure out why this keeps happening."

Result: "The good news is that we found the process flaw and there is a systems fix we can make to correct it permanently. Miranda said Carmen is willing to give us another chance, and we really believe we can satisfy her."

Support Needed: "I think it would go a long way to have you, the head of the department, call her personally and give her our assurance."

The final prep step for SAR(s) is to write down the anticipated question and your answer, and practice your answer out loud using a stopwatch. Typically most SAR(s) statements last between thirty and ninety seconds. (Chuck's statement above runs about thirty-five seconds.) The amount of detail is a decision you will have to make based on your knowledge of the person asking the question.

Now I know SAR(s) is also the name of a highly contagious disease, but that makes it easy to remember. You may have noticed its familiar structure too: it's basically the what, how, and why.

Simple structure and a simple process: In advance, anticipate who will you run into and what will he ask you, and write your SAR(s) answer down. Then practice. That's it.

The more you practice this, the easier it gets. Eventually you will get so good at this that when you spot someone heading toward your elevator, you can anticipate the potential question and start drafting the answer in your head.

Let's practice the technique.

Step one: Think about the projects and activities that are keeping you busy at work right now.

➲ What are you presently working on that people might ask you about?

➲ Who might you run into over the next few days that might want a quick update from you on a certain project or activity?

Make a few notes below:

Who I might run into:

_____

What they might ask me:

_____

_____

_____

Step two: Construct your answer using the SAR(s) model *(see next page).*

Situation/status:

Actions taken or planned:

Result/response expected:

(Support needed, if any):

Step three: Rehearse your statement out loud and time it. Go back and do a little trimming if it seems overly wordy. If you can record yourself and play it back, listen and give yourself a little feedback:

- ⤷ Does your message flow? Is it logical?

- ⤷ Is it concise and still complete?

- ⤷ Is the amount of detail relevant for the asker? (Don't overtalk; the questioner can always ask for more detail if she wants it.)

Pretty simple, right? Imagine if you did this preparation with some regularity: what would be the impact on your ability to manage these moments? What would it say about your presence?

_____

_____

Yes, you would appear more polished and prepared because you *are* more prepared!

◆

Let's get back to Delia. I wanted to help her turn her SAR(s) prep into a habit, so each Friday she would prepare her SAR(s) statements for the next week and we would practice them on the phone for fifteen minutes. We would trim and refine, and then Delia would continue to practice them over the weekend. She would rehearse them out loud while driving to the market, or say them to herself while riding the subway, so that on Monday she felt ready for whomever she met in the elevator. Her confidence increased with each interaction, and before long Delia didn't need our Friday calls anymore. She knew how to organize her thoughts quickly due to her preparation and practice, and her confidence increased dramatically. This, together with the focus on other elements of her presence, helped her win that promotion at last.

"Once Upon a Time There Was a Roast Beef ..."

Stories are amazing unifiers. Every family has them; every culture has them, and we learn to love stories as small children. When my nephew was a toddler, all I had to do was say in a tempting voice: "Once upon a time …" and he would run to our "story place" and wiggle in excitement, waiting to hear the next adventure.

On some level, we still respond that way. When presenters want to establish their presence, engage their audience, introduce the theme, and relax, they use an opening anecdote (as shown in our presentation model on page 171.) No, we don't mean a joke. We mean a story. We sometimes refer to the opening and closing stories as "The Wrapper" because they wrap around your prepared content. Your wrapper might be an anecdote from your personal experience, or it might be a relevant item from the news. Regardless, its purpose is to engage and connect with the audience.

> There's an old myth that one should open a presentation with a joke. This was a big idea in the 1950s and 1960s and folks who did public speaking at that time owned and wrote books filled with jokes for every occasion. Thank goodness that trend has passed! These days, a heartfelt story or anecdote will help you connect with your audience in ways that jokes never will. One more caution: You have to be really sure of your audience before you use any joke to ensure you don't inadvertently offend someone.

A good story or anecdote doesn't have to be long. I've heard great ones that last less than a minute. A story works when:

- ➲ It is relevant to the topic and the audience.

- ➲ It is well told, with clear forward momentum and without tangents or explanations.

- ⮎ It is a sensory experience, sprinkled with words that help us see, hear, and even smell what was going on.

- ⮎ The presenter is personally involved in the story in some way. The story doesn't have to be about the presenter, although that can work well, but the presenter needs to be a part of it in some way (see box on page 188).

Leaders who are effective communicators understand the power of stories and use them well. They know:

- ⮎ People need context. Stories provide a framework for understanding because they reveal familiar patterns (example: "The Boy Who Cried Wolf").

- ⮎ Stories are engaging; we all want to know how it turns out!

- ⮎ Good stories are memorable, vivid, easy to remember and retell.

- ⮎ Stories connect to people's emotions, and thus to their energy, and presence is all about connecting.

Stories have a subtle power. Annette Simmons, author of *The Story Factor*, says that stories are an effective method of influence. "Persuasion … is a push strategy. Story is a pull strategy. If your story is good enough, people—of their own free will—come to the conclusion they can trust you and the message you bring."[21]

Stories are efficient. It seems counterintuitive to think that if I add a story, I can actually trim the amount of overall content, but that's often what happens. When the story's theme or characters are well known, referring to them can make the point more quickly and effectively than any amount of business-speak verbiage. For example, by simply saying "The emperor has no clothes here," we describe the problem (that our leader is isolated from the truth of the current situation and no one has figured out a way to tell him what's really going on)—in only six words.

Stories inspire us. Hollywood screenwriter William McKee, author of the Harvard Business Review article "Storytelling That Moves People," says that stories speak to us because we often feel like the protagonist in any epic. We set off on our quest or mission with zeal and focus, get knocked off our horse by the dragon du jour, fight evil, rescue the helpless, and hopefully climb back on our noble steed and ride off into the sunset—every day. In the telling of any heroic tale, when we identify with the protagonist and he wins the day, we feel it is possible that we can win the day. I once had an employee say aloud at a meeting the theme from the story of *The Little Engine That Could*: "I think I can, I think I can," and we all knew exactly what she meant.

Stories are memorable. Here is a story that one of my former CEOs told at the start of a meeting of the company's officers many years ago, and I still remember it clearly:

> *When I was newly married, I noticed that my bride cut the two ends off of a roast beef before she put it in the oven. Now, meat was expensive and we were on a newlywed's budget, so I didn't like to see the waste, but what did I know about cooking a roast? So I asked her why she did that, and she replied, "Because my mother always did it." Okay ... so the next time I saw my mother-in-law, I very diplomatically asked her why she cut the ends off of her roast beef, and she said, "Because*

my mother always did it." Hmm ... now I was really curious. So over the holidays when we saw my wife's grandmother, I asked her why she cut the ends off of her roast beef. "Oh," she said, "When I was newly married, our first apartment had such a tiny oven that it was the only way I could fit the roast into the pan. Then it just became a habit."

Our CEO chose that story because our company was about to make a very dramatic change in our operating structure that would significantly alter the way we ran our businesses. Every single person in the organization was going to have to look at the way we did our work every day, and ask if this was really the best way to do it. It was no longer going to be acceptable or even feasible to do things because "that's the way we always did them before." The CEO used this engaging, one-minute story to introduce the theme for the entire meeting, and I still remember how it made me feel many years later.

As you go to various meetings, start to notice which speakers use stories well. It is likely that these speakers have been using stories all along, but they do it so effortlessly that you never really noticed it as a specific technique.

Ultimately, using an opening anecdote to lead into your content achieves three things:

1. It connects the audience to you through emotion, engaging both the head and the heart.

2. It sets up the theme of your presentation and prepares people to listen.

3. It relaxes you through the initial adrenalin rush most speakers feel for the first minute or so of their presentation.

How to Start a Story

Notice in these story starters the presenters aren't always making the story about themselves, but they are involved in some way. For instance, they could share a story that was told to them. Try creating your own anecdote using one of these openers, customizing it for your reality:

- As I was preparing for this meeting, I recalled my first encounter with ...

- Two weeks ago, I had the opportunity to spend time with our leader. He told me about a time when he ...

- One of the toughest situations I had to face as a young engineer was ...

- When my daughter was only five years old, she taught me a very important lesson ...

- One of the ways I like to spend my free time is (hobby) because it gives me the opportunity to interact with interesting people. Just last week, one of our club members shared this experience ...

- Like many of us, I didn't grow up dreaming to be a part of this industry. However, when I was just nineteen years old, I learned an important lesson that really changed my career plans and stays with me to this day ...

- At our offsite meeting last month, a young employee in my organization introduced herself to me, and we started talking. She told me something quite interesting ...

- The previous speaker referred to the plans for (Project X), and I recalled a time several years ago when we were launching (Project Z), which is now our fastest growing product segment. I remember sitting with the team, however, worrying we would never hit the launch date, when one fellow said ...

The recurring theme in the box above is that all of the "story starters" refer to a specific situation, or to an event that really happened. When stories are personal and specific, they are far more engaging. I've seen this in action many times. For instance, in our presence and presentation skills seminars the participants have to develop a five-minute presentation to deliver in class and they are required to put a personal anecdote in there somewhere. After the presentation, their classmates and I give them feedback on their performance. Observers are specifically asked to comment on any point in the presentation where they were most engaged or where they felt their interest fade out. In the vast majority of the presentations, the observers felt most engaged when the presenters shared their personal anecdotes. Observers also noticed that the presenter was more alive when he or she talked about something personal. Obviously there is something meaningful for the speaker behind the story, and those emotions flavor the story in a way that is quite compelling to the audience.

> *Good presenters keep a file of stories that always work for them. They practice them and use them as needed to make their content come alive.*

Managing Nerves When Communicating

Public speaking continues to be high on the list of things that people fear. If you flipped to this section before reading anything else in the book, it is likely high on your list too. You might be nervous about making a formal presentation in front of a large audience, or you might worry about speaking up in a meeting of your peers. In coaching leaders, I've learned that there are lots of reasons why people feel nervous when speaking in public. Some people had a traumatic experience early in their career that keeps haunting them; some describe themselves as shy or introverted and declare public speaking to be "against their nature," and some suffer from what psychologists call evaluation apprehension, or the fear of looking stupid.[22] Believe me, I understand that fear too. Like most fears, we may not be able to erase its root cause, but we can manage our response to the fear-inducing trigger. Keep in mind that leaders must demonstrate courage, so dig deep and get ready to tackle the nervousness that sometimes accompanies public speaking.

There are effective techniques for managing nerves before and during presentations. However, which technique will work for you depends on the nature of your nervousness.

Let's begin with your self-awareness. How do you feel just before it's your turn to present at a meeting? What emotions do you experience, and what bodily responses do you notice?

_____

_____

_____

_____

Your emotions, triggered by the rush of adrenalin, likely include excitement, fear, pleasure, anxiety, or maybe a little bit of all of them. These emotions likely show up in your body as:

➲ Rapid heart rate or pounding in the ears

➲ Shallow breathing

- ➲ Red face

- ➲ Sweaty palms

- ➲ Butterflies in the tummy

- ➲ Tension in legs or shoulders

- ➲ Rocking or pacing with no real destination

- ➲ Use of filler ("um," "uh")

- ➲ Blank mind, inability to remember your words for a moment

Does this list sound familiar? You saw most of these items listed in Chapter Three when we talked about fight, flight, or freeze and the amygdala hijack. If you skipped that chapter, please read pages 88–99 for some important background on the neuroscience behind this physiological response, but for now the important thing to know is this: You can calm yourself by taking several long, slow deep breaths before beginning your presentation in order to slow your heart rate and calm your brain. This is known as the **"studied breath"** because you are paying attention to your breath as a means of getting centered and grounded.[23]

We introduced the technique of deep breaths in Chapter Three. You did an exercise to help you understand exactly what your hot buttons are so you could avoid moments of personal regret. The same principle applies here: it's important to know exactly what we're afraid of regarding public speaking so we know what to do about it. For example:

I'm anxious about public speaking because...	Possible Remedies
I have too much material and they'll cut me off.	Practice out loud and time yourself. Then trim your content until you come in at 75 percent of the time allowed.
I'm afraid they'll think my presentation is boring.	Use an opening anecdote that will resonate with the audience; build in opportunities for audience interaction; select only those headlines and details that are most interesting to the audience; tap into your own passion for the topic and let that show.
I will forget to say an important point or lose my place.	Practice several times out loud and/or record yourself and listen to it several times so your content is really familiar; use minimal notes and highlight sparingly so when you glance at your notes it's easy to find your spot. Remember leaders are resilient; if you lose your place you will recover and carry on.
Someone will ask me a question that I can't answer.	Anticipate questions (see page 172) and research and write down your answers; brainstorm with knowledgeable colleagues about questions this audience might have; allow yourself to say you don't know but will find out.
People will notice my hands are shaking and they'll know I'm anxious.	Long slow deep breaths will calm you all over. Shake your hands vigorously at the wrists for twenty to thirty seconds before going to the meeting room; be sure your notes are secured to a firm backing so your paper doesn't flutter; compensate with strong eye contact and a confident voice.

Finally, it's possible that you aren't really nervous at all; you're just excited. The flush of adrenalin and other bodily responses feel very similar whether we are afraid or excited. If you've conquered the list above and you still feel your heart race and your palms sweat just before a presentation, relax and breathe; you're just excited.

What are some other ways to use up some of that excess energy?

- ⮩ One client of mine closes her office door, kicks off her shoes, and does jumping jacks.

- ⮩ Another client makes sure he gets on his treadmill that morning for at least one mile.

- ⮩ If nerves make your mouth dry, be sure to bring a half-glass of water up with you, just enough to wet your lips during a pause. In my experience, just having the water there helps you relax and you might not even need it. And don't forget those deep breaths that relax you too.

Here's another hint: Earlier in this chapter we mentioned that using a story or anecdote at the start of a presentation brings the added benefit of relaxing the speaker. Most speakers who experience only mild stage fright calm down a minute or two into their presentation, and so the opening wrapper acts as a safe emotional bridge to get them to their main content.

◆

Listening and Responding Actively

Active listening is a generic phrase used to describe the behavior exhibited by one person listening to another person such that the speaker sees and hears acknowledgement from the listener. For instance, the speaker might see the listener nod her head or take a note. The speaker might hear the listener say "Mm-hm," or "Tell me more." Active listening is an important part of presence because it's the one form of listening in which your conversational partner knows you are listening. You show you are listening by the nonverbal signals you send and, of course, by how you respond to the speaker.

There is a specific form of active listening that applies during the Q&A part of a presentation that is called the *active listening and responding technique*. This technique is ideal for answering relatively routine questions during or after a presentation, but it can be useful any time because it:

- ➲ Helps the listener hear the question and organize a response more readily;

- ➲ Demonstrates to the asker that the question was heard;

- ➲ Allows answers to be prepared in advance when coupled with the anticipatory questions technique.

How do you typically feel during the Q&A part of your presentation?

(a) I prefer it to the formal remarks. I like the informal nature of the Q&A.

(b) I dread it much more than the formal remarks because you never know what someone will ask you.

(c) I'm fine with it. No issues.

If you answered (b) you might feel anxious because you haven't yet built the habit of anticipatory questions (see page 173) or you don't practice Q&A enough. However, another reason is that you're experiencing both fear and excitement, as we discussed on page 190. When you focus so much on your presentation and putting your content out there in the way you rehearsed and planned, it can be difficult to refocus on what's coming at you in the form of questions, especially if you are still on that adrenalin high of the presentation. Remember, the adrenalin makes it hard to focus at times. However, with the technique below, you can focus your attention in such a way that the answer will come more readily to you.

The Knee Bone's Connected to the Thigh Bone...

First, let's look at the basic anatomy of a question: Every question has a head and a tail, as shown in the diagram on page 196. The head of the question can be minimal, but often in business presentations it is long and hard to follow because the asker is using the Q&A as an opportunity to voice an opinion, grandstand, think out loud, and occasionally to begin his question. The problem for presenters is that if this preface goes on too long, they begin to wonder: "where the heck is the question?"

The question comes in the tail and usually starts when we hear typical interrogatives such as why, who, when, how, did you, couldn't we, shouldn't they, and so forth. These are the *signal words* that tell us a question is coming.

The active listening and responding technique requires you to use two or three of the questioner's exact words to start your answer. We call these the *operative words*, because they are the engines driving the actual question. They often stand out, because they reflect the questioner's intent, emotion, or bias. One operative word will always be a verb. The other will be a provocative or distinctive word. You need to listen for these words which will come quickly after the signal words.

Most questions reflect this basic anatomy; some may include a long editorial, others a short one or none at all.

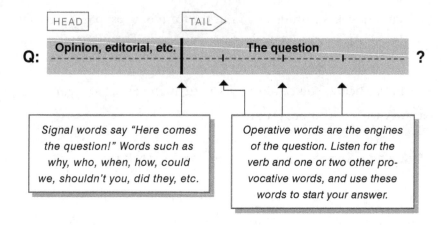

Five Steps for Active Listening and Responding

1. Stay present throughout the asking of the question. Take steady, calming breaths to maintain your poise and use subtle body language that says, "I'm listening."

2. Listen for the two or three exact operative words that follow the signal words as shown in the diagram above.

3. Pause briefly to be sure you don't jump in too quickly. Then begin your answer using the asker's exact operative words without parroting the question, maintaining eye contact with the asker through the first part of your answer.[24]

4. Proceed to answer the question using the word "and" (not "but") to connect back to something in your presentation.

5. Provide just enough detail to support your answer, being careful not to overanswer the question.

This basic structure allows you to stay in the moment, but it takes some practice. See if you can find the signal word and operative words in the example below. Suppose you just did a presentation on budget cuts using your KMH model, and someone asks you this question:

Q: You said earlier that these budget cuts would be allocated between the different lines of business, but some lines are already underfunded and understaffed, so I was wondering how the allocations will be managed so that those businesses can still move toward recovery?

A: One of the ways to *manage* the *recovery* in those lines is to provide an investment from the other lines so they can get the staff and equipment they need, and so the *allocations* will reflect the conditions in each business line. For example…

Signal word "how"; operative words "manage" (verb) "recovery" and "allocations."

This technique ensures that the person asking the question feels heard because he literally hears his own words coming back at him. It also helps the presenter maintain poise and presence because the questioner's words help her start her answer, and then she can link back to her key message.

Sometimes the head of the question is very short or even nonexistent: the asker starts immediately with the signal words. Sometimes the head is so long you wonder if you're ever going to hear a question. In the latter case, you really need to stay centered and focused, using the studied breath to stay present and patient. I recommend practicing active listening when you are not under pressure. For instance, you can practice listening for the signal and operative words during any meeting or during part of a conference call where you are in a relatively passive role. Pay attention when someone asks a question, and see if you can spot the signal and operational words. Once you grasp the concept, you can practice the active responding technique silently in your head or on your paper.

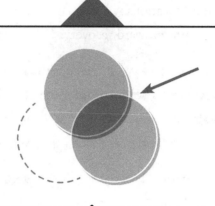

In our presence model, the overlap between the top and right circles is devoted to "speaking with authority." When we are clear on our strengths and confident in our knowledge, and when we can express ourselves through clear, commanding communication, then we can speak with authority.

Also in this overlap is "managing feelings so they are expressed appropriately." This means having the self-awareness to know how we feel about something, and the courage and skill to express it authentically.

Finally, this section of the model includes "listening without bias." With self-awareness, we can recognize our own biases and predispositions and make the effort to listen openly.

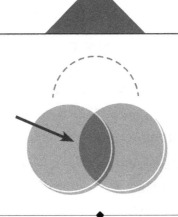

In our presence model, the overlap between the left and right circles is devoted to "sharing openly while respecting listeners' time, level, interests, and needs." Senior-level people complain that junior people give them way too much information. They want their updates high level and brief. Meanwhile, junior people tell me they wish senior people would give them more information. They are hungry for more direction, strategic insight, and rationale. Interpersonal awareness means tuning in to others' needs and then communicating in the way that they want.

MOMENT TO
REFLECT

- ❑ All communication is presence in action. Managing the essential elements of look, sound, and content helps you come across the way you want to come across every time.

- ❑ Don't shortchange yourself when it comes to preparation. Even routine presentations are opportunities.

- ❑ Clarity of purpose around communication means knowing what you want people to think, feel or do as a result of your presentation. Purpose is driven by the emotions of both the speaker and the audience.

- ❑ Every message should contain the "what, how and why" to be complete.

- ❑ The key message-headline model ensures your communiqué will be well organized and complete without being overly long because its preparation is based on the available time for the presentation and the needs of the audience.

- ❑ Both the anticipatory questions and the SAR(s) technique can help you prepare for the unexpected so that you appear poised, prepared, and present.

- ❑ Stories help people connect to your message—and to you.

- ❑ There are techniques that help reduce the nervousness that can hinder presentations.

- ❑ Active listening and responding assures others that their questions are truly heard, and helps the speaker formulate a clear answer quickly.

6

PRESENCE AND YOUR BRAND: HOW DO YOU WANT TO BE KNOWN?

I was a late bloomer.

In my twenties I tried a little bit of everything from professional singer to substitute teacher to actor. I even worked for a time as the rush-hour traffic reporter for an oldies radio station. I also spent six years working for one of the largest insurance companies in the country. Some of you may recall that in the late 1970s women were just starting to enter the workforce in large numbers. In fact, I was part of the first training class of underwriter trainees that was deliberately filled with 50 percent men and 50 percent women. Let me tell you, the women felt very self-conscious. It seemed as if everyone was watching us to see if this whole women-at-work thing was going to work out.

Meanwhile, we were looking around to figure out how we were supposed to act. What were the rules? How were things negotiated internally? How were decisions really made? Who got listened to at meetings, and why? And even...how should we dress? (Ladies, remember those little silk bow ties we wore? Our version of their corporate uniform.) To complicate matters, there weren't a lot of professional suits and dresses to choose from back then, especially for women under 5'4" (like me) so there weren't many choices even if one did have an image in mind. There were no female directors in our division at that time, so there weren't even role models for us to emulate, and there was no one in a position of authority who looked like me. In spite of my solid education, decent analytical skills, and intelligence, I felt awkward and self-conscious. I felt very much like a little girl with big blue eyes and a squeaky voice and a bow tie, trying to be taken seriously. Even though I came armed with a strong work ethic and the desire to succeed, after a couple of promotions I reached a dead end, and when my job was eliminated, I happily took the severance package and ran.

That severance period ended up being a great time for reflection. I continued to work as an actor and singer, but found I missed the intellectual challenge (and the paycheck) that came from working in business. So when an opportunity came up to join another insurance company in a really interesting position, I took it. But before I started, I decided to change some things. I didn't want to be the shy little girl with the big blue eyes and the squeaky voice any more. I wanted to be a confident, successful, professional woman who was recognized for adding value to her company every day. So:

- I changed my hair.

- I changed my walk.

- I changed my voice.

- I got a few good suits and a really good tailor.

- I built a peer network as quickly as I could.

- I had a point of view.

Every day as I walked into our suburban office building, I could see my reflection in the plate-glass windows, and I would square my shoulders, lengthen my stride, and walk in the door with my "bring-it!" face. I was going to appear confident even if it wasn't quite true —yet. But I was putting those data points out every day, consistently, hoping I could show on the outside what I knew I was capable of on the inside.

And guess what? It worked. As I appeared more confident, I was given more opportunities. In turn, each success brought me more confidence, and so the cycle continued. I knew my "branding" mission was successful when it was announced in the company newsletter that I was promoted to director, and one of the department heads came over to me and said, "I was really surprised to see that you were promoted to director."

"You were?" I replied, bracing myself for teasing, or worse.

"Yes," he said. "I thought you already were a director. After all, you walk around here like you own the place."

Mission accomplished.

◆

Let's Give 'Em Something to Talk About

Who decides how you are perceived? You do, through your actions and behaviors. If you've read this book straight through from the beginning, you've seen the phrase "data points" many times. If you are jumping around and started with this chapter, this is what you need to know to catch up:

1. Every action or behavior is a data point.

2. Every interaction contains multiple data points.

3. Data points are connected into patterns that become "the truth" about you from an observer's point of view.

4. *You* own your data points, and therefore you can influence how you are perceived.

Let's face it, people are already talking about you. The people above you are discussing your merits (you hope!) in the quarterly talent review or in planning meetings; your coworkers are critiquing your performance based on what they observe at a meeting; and your direct reports are talking about you all the time just because you are the boss.

Don't you wonder what they are saying?

Sometimes reputations are built accidentally. People put data points out there without thinking about how others might connect the dots, like Marvin in Chapter Two and like me in my first job. We want to build our reputations purposefully, which is what I did in my next job and have continued to do purposefully since then. You can do it too. This chapter completes the right circle in our presence model and is devoted to *taking charge of your brand*, making clear crisp choices about how you want to be known, and then making that come true through your specific actions and behaviors.

Heads Up's Presence Model: Communication and Brand, Part 2

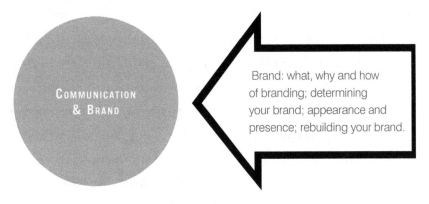

COMMUNICATION & BRAND

Brand: what, why and how of branding; determining your brand; appearance and presence; rebuilding your brand.

Brand:

- ➲ The what, why and how of branding
- ➲ Determining your brand
- ➲ Appearance and presence
- ➲ Rebuilding your brand

The What, Why and How of Branding

Let's begin with the idea of a brand. We're all familiar with iconic brands, so in your own words, what is a brand? What is its purpose?

_____

_____

_____

_____

The word "brand" originally referred to the mark made by a hot iron to allow ranchers to identify their own cattle. Over time, brands became identified with various companies, products, or services to allow consumers to distinguish one over the other. Well-established companies rely on their brand and reputation to help them weather challenging times; during good times they work hard to reinforce the positive aspects of their brand so that over time the brand supports them and they support the brand. The word "brand," according to *Wikipedia*, "has continued to evolve to encompass identity … It is defined by a perception, good or bad, that your customers or prospects have about you." Therefore, if brand is defined by people's perceptions, it follows that in order to create or enhance our brand we, like good marketers, have to *put the data points out there that will influence perception.*

"But why?" you might be asking yourself. "Why should I invest time and energy in branding? My boss already knows I do a good job, and a good job speaks for itself." Sorry, but that idea is naïve and outdated. We aren't arguing the "good job" part, just the part about "speaking for itself." We live in the information age. We are inundated with information from every possible source during every waking minute of our day. Everything from billboards to beeping IM alerts screams "Notice me! Pay attention to me!" and we do our best to sort it all out. So that poor little "job speaking for itself" is easily drowned out, unheard, and possibly unnoticed.

Thus, the first reason to create your brand is to help you stand out in all that noise. Watch your boss for a couple of days. Is she sitting around with lots of time on her hands and nothing else to think about but l'il ole you? Not likely. Your branding efforts will help her and all your key stakeholders cut through the clutter. If they are going to talk about you, make it easy for their internal storage and retrieval system to find the right words to say.

The second reason to brand yourself is to help you stand out in the way you want to be known. Going through this effort gives you clarity around who you are, what you stand for, and how you and your team add value every day. When *you* are crystal clear on how you want to be known, it is less likely that you will inadvertently send out vague or incompatible messages.

ACTIVITY

Look at this scenario and answer the three questions below:

Tina is a very conscientious first-level manager. She oversees her team carefully to ensure that all the big things and little tasks get done, and things always get done even if she occasionally has to do them herself. She diligently reports the particulars of these accomplishments in her weekly report at her boss's staff meeting. Her peers are often surprised at her grasp of the details for work completed by someone on her team. She hopes her boss

will see her specificity as proof that she has mastered the
details and is ready to move up to the next level.

1. **How do you think Tina's boss and peers see her? Choose one:**

    a. Detail-oriented and tactical

    b. A micromanager

    c. A good manager

    You might have chosen (a) because if you look carefully at the scenario, this is what Tina is telling them about herself week after week through her words and deeds. But wait a minute. Is this what Tina has in mind?

2. **How do you think Tina sees herself—as a, b, or c?**

    Right, she probably sees herself as (c)—a good manager. After all, she ensures that things get done even if she has to roll up her sleeves and do them herself. But we all know that the higher level skill is to develop and delegate, so she is actually working against herself here if she want to be promoted.

3. **Now suppose Tina has someone on her team who likes to work independently. How would he see her—as a, b, or c?**

    Yes, he would likely see her as (b)—a micromanager, and depending on how strongly he feels, this is the way that he will talk about Tina to others. In other words, this is how a perception or misperception about her brand will spread.

    What Tina hasn't figured out yet is that people will draw conclusions based on the data points she gives them, and they will connect the dots in the way that makes sense to them. If Tina aspires to reach a higher level in the organization, she will have to learn to highlight different aspects of her skills and achievements and put new data points out there to ensure people perceive her the way she wants to be perceived. Here's an activity that she—and *you*—can use to get there.

Aspirational Adjectives Activity

This activity helps you decide how you want to be known, and then create the data points that influence the way that others see you—and talk about you.

First, make a list of "aspirational adjectives," which would be those words that you wish or hope people use to describe you at work. These adjectives might be true now; people actually use these words to describe you, or they might be somewhat aspirational in that they aren't true yet, but you're working on them.

In any order, please list eight to ten adjectives:

1. _____   6. _____

2. _____   7. _____

3. _____   8. _____

4. _____   9. _____

5. _____   10. _____

I'll bet the first four or five came quickly, and the others took a little longer. It's worth pushing yourself to come up with at least ten words because most people put the easy ones first (see box).

Stuck? Take your time and keep thinking. If your list is still a little short, think about your own greatness, and see if you can find a word to describe yourself without the limits of self-consciousness. What values are important to you, and how would people describe someone who demonstrates those values? Another way to stretch yourself on this list is to think of someone you admire and would like to emulate. What words would you use to describe that person that you hope people will use to describe you someday? When you move beyond the obvious ones, you start to imagine who you can be in your own future.

Now that you have brainstormed ten adjectives, let's begin to narrow down your branding efforts. Sure, in time people may use all ten of those words to describe you, but for this activity we need to trim the list. How? First review the list and look for items that are similar or duplicative, such as "smart" and "intelligent," or "collaborative" and "team player." Eliminate the duplicates, then add any new adjectives so you still have eight to ten. Think hard. Choose words that describe what is distinctive or special about you. Be strategic and pick words that help people see your unique strengths more clearly.

Next, with these thoughts in mind, choose three adjectives from your list that you feel are most critical to your brand right now:

1.

2.

3.

These three words will help you build and clarify your brand over the next six to twelve months. Let's start with one word to show you how, and then you can apply the process to the other two words over the next six to twelve months.

From your list of three, choose one adjective to apply in this activity: _____

In the space below, list as many actions and behaviors you can think of that are representative of that adjective. What do you do, or what do you see other people do, or what do you hear them say when you or they are demonstrating that adjective?

_____

_____

_____

_____

_____

◆

In this activity, you are making decisions about how your brand is going to appear to other people. You see, for a brand to be successful, *we have to show people who we are through our behavior.* But showing them isn't enough by itself. We also have to tell them what they are seeing—that is, give them a label for that behavior so they know how to categorize it in their heads. And then, like all good marketers, we have to repeat the message. We have to tell them again, and show them some more, and tell them again, and show them some more … like this:

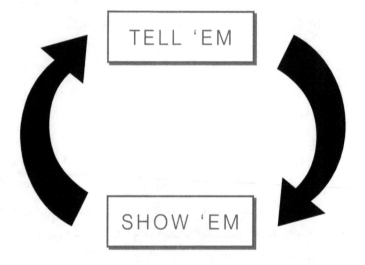

Remember, one of our objectives in branding is to cut through the clutter of information people receive and make it easy for them to talk about us in the way we want, and that takes repetition.

Here's an example to show you how the cycle works. Let's start with "show 'em." Suppose one of your critical aspirational adjectives is "confident." You believe that you are confident on the inside, but you've gotten some feedback that you need to display more confidence at work.

What actions or behaviors would we notice in someone that would cause us to say that person is confident?

- ⮑ Great eye contact

- ⮑ Stands tall, good posture

- ⮑ Clear speaking voice

- ⮑ Has a point of view and isn't afraid to share it

- ⮑ Open to good debate, not threatened by others' perspectives

- ⮑ Comfortable speaking in front of groups of people

- ⮑ Smiles easily

- ⮑ Firm handshake

- ⮑ Is direct (and fair) with feedback

Suppose I meet someone and notice that she displays all of the behaviors in that list. I might describe her as experienced, assured, proud, or even leader-like. Those are all great words, but they aren't the branding word. The branding word in this example is "confident." So how do we get people to use *that* word? How? By using the word ourselves in our everyday language so we become associated with that word. By everyday language I mean literally the kinds of conversations you have every day at work. I don't mean talking *about* your word. I mean using the word itself as a part of your regular work conversations. Find ways to use your branding word as much as you can. Use it to describe other people. Use it to answer a question. Use it about yourself when it makes sense. Use it any time you might have used a different word or phrase to say the same thing so that people start to associate you with the word. For example:

- "I really like working with Shakti. She is enthusiastic and confident and that rubs off on the whole team" (as opposed to "She is enthusiastic and has a can-do attitude that …").

- "Yes, we are confident that we can hit the deadline" (as opposed to "Yes, we'll hit the deadline").

- "Of the two potential candidates for the open position, Ethan seemed more confident, perhaps because of his experience at XYZ company" (as opposed to "Ethan seemed more sure of himself because of …").

Same meaning, just a deliberate use of the word.

The idea behind the tell-'em-show-'em branding cycle is a simple one: you are (or are working toward) displaying those behaviors and you're putting a label on them so that people actually see them for what they are. But here's the rule: You can't just paste a label on something if it isn't there or isn't true. Your branding word has to be true. It had better show up in your words and your deeds.

I once worked with a woman who consistently described herself as a team player but whose behavior was competitive and exclusionary. The fact that she was trying to label herself as something different undermined her credibility with her peers tremendously. If she had said, "Hey, I'm competitive! It's a dog-eat-dog world." she might have had more credibility with her colleagues. So if you're using "the word," it had better be true!

Let's try this and help Tina out from the story on page 207. Tina has decided that her top three aspirational adjectives are "strategic," "organized," and "responsible." Which one should she choose?

- ⮑ We already know that she is *organized*; that is a clear strength that no one would question.

- ⮑ She wants to be seen as *strategic*, but that one is purely aspirational at this point in time. She will need to start demonstrating more strategic behaviors before she can use the branding word "strategic" with any credibility.

- ⮑ We also know that she does not shy away from *responsibility*, but her opportunity in this case is to demonstrate the competency at a higher level, away from the details and definitely away from doing the job herself, so this is partly a strength but also partly aspirational.

Tina has decided to brand herself as *responsible*. What are the actions and behaviors of a middle manager who is responsible?

_____

_____

_____

A responsible middle manager is one who:

- ⮑ Ensures the work gets done through other people;

⮑ Holds herself and her people accountable for performance;

⮑ Develops and mentors people to enable them to reach their full potential;

⮑ Reports on progress, success, and failure to the management team above her in an objective, concise, and audience-centric manner.

If she displays the above behaviors, Tina could cement her brand by using the words "responsible" or "responsibility" in everyday sentences like these:

- I'm happy to say that Kendall was fully responsible for that terrific outcome.

- Yes, the team knows that they are responsible for hitting the deadline, and so...

- We're ready to promote Axel. He is knowledgeable, creative and has a strong sense of responsibility for outcomes...

- I'll take responsibility for ensuring that the team delivers on...

Now, back to your brand: Using the adjective that you chose as critical, write down some everyday sentences where you can use your word. Then, try saying those sentences out loud. This is an important step, because if the word feels awkward in your speaking vocabulary, you won't use it every day. If that's the case, find an easier-to-speak synonym that describes those same behaviors and develop that as your branding word.

Everyday sentences for your branding adjective:

_____

_____

_____

_____◆_____

The more you use the word and demonstrate the behavior, the more people will start to see you the way you want to be seen. You can build your image one aspirational adjective at a time. Be patient and persistent. It may take several months for the word to take hold, but you'll know it's working when you hear the word coming back at you. Then you can layer on another aspirational adjective from your list.

Extra Hint: Apply Branding to SAR(s)

In Chapter Five you learned the SAR(s) model, useful for anticipating and preparing for potential surprise questions in the hallway or cafeteria. When you are preparing your SAR(s) statements, be sure to include your branding word somewhere.

For instance, Tina might be stopped in the hallway and she responds to a question by saying:

S: Yes, Friday's meeting regarding the rewrites was a long one, but was ultimately successful.

A: We mapped out the next steps and got a commitment from everyone that people would turn around their changes in twenty-four hours.

R: It's great that everyone is taking responsibility for the deadline. I feel confident that we can still meet the printing date of the thirty-first of the month.

My Brand

Remember the story of my early days in corporate America from the start of this chapter? You might be wondering how and why I made the changes I did. At the time, my aspirational adjectives were "confident," "knowledgeable," and "collaborative." So I spent some time thinking about these three adjectives. What does "confident" look like and sound like? Who looks or sounds confident to me, and why is that? I did the same thing with my other adjectives, and I paid attention to people on television, in the movies, and even on the street, and I noticed their specific actions and behaviors, which helped me create my own to-do list:

- ⮎ I changed my hair to appear less mousy. I chose a style that was more current and less "safe" to demonstrate that I wasn't afraid of change. It was the mid-1980s, and big hair was the style, so I went big. (Big shoulder pads too, as on TV's *Dallas* and *Designing Women*.)

- ⮎ I changed my walk by lengthening my stride, again to appear more confident. Remember the print ads for Charlie perfume by Revlon? They always pictured a confident young woman with a long stride. I decided to try that, too.

- ⮎ I changed my speaking voice, using the deeper notes in my range and emphasizing my diction so that my voice sounded more authoritative. I was lucky to be on the radio just prior to this job change, so I had lots of tape to play back and critique myself. I practiced constantly. I noticed when I got excited, my voice slipped back to the higher part of the range, so I had to be even more self-aware during those times.

⮑ I got a few good suits and a really good tailor. As I said, it was difficult to find professional clothes in my size, but I focused on a few really good things and paid to have them altered. It was worth it, because when I wore those things I felt confident. I still work with a personal shopper to help me make bolder choices for special work situations.

⮑ I built a peer network as quickly as I could. In my first few weeks with the company, I asked my boss which coworkers I should meet in order to be effective with my assignments. I called everyone on that list and set up coffee or lunch meetings, and I built rapport with all of them. Having lots of new friends spread across the division made me feel more knowledgeable and more confident. It also showed I was a collaborative team player. My boss said he never saw anyone build a network as quickly and effectively as I did. (He didn't know I was a woman on a mission!)

⮑ I had a point of view. Even though I looked and sounded mousy in my previous job, I did gain exceptionally good experience. It was entirely appropriate for me to have a point of view on matters within my area of expertise. I practiced starting sentences with "in my experience" or "from what I've seen" and thought carefully about how I wanted to articulate my opinions. My goal was to demonstrate knowledge, yes, but also to build bridges with my new teammates, so I didn't want to sound too arrogant. In my old job, I was comfortable just sitting back and listening to what others had to say, but in this new job, I wanted my voice to be heard, so I made sure I was ready.

I was lucky to have the chance to reinvent myself as I moved to my new company, but you don't need to change companies to start fresh. You can apply these branding techniques right now and create the future you want to create for yourself.

"Dress to Impress": Appearance and Presence

Companies spend millions on packaging for their products, knowing that an appealing wrapper will help consumers cut through the clutter of similar products on the shelves and choose theirs. Packaging also reflects the unique value of that brand. For example, when I purchased my first Apple product, an iPod, the elegantly spare and simple packaging told me it was going to be easy to use—and it was. I was up and humming in less than five minutes.

And yes, people do judge a book by its cover. *The Harvard Business Review's* article "Hot or Not?" asks the question of whether physical appearance and attractiveness is a topic that managers should take seriously. The article goes on to tell us about studies showing that hiring managers demonstrate "preferences for hiring poorly qualified, well-groomed job candidates over well-qualified, poorly groomed ones."[25] So, like it or not, appearances do matter and on some level we all know that. It matters to you: Have you ever noticed that when you know you look really good, your confidence is a little higher? And it matters to your colleagues, too: I recently worked with a really capable new CEO, and on his 360° feedback report one of his direct reports said, "He is a true professional, even in the way he dresses he shows he cares. His shoes are always shined. (Yes, we notice.)"

Clothing is linked to credibility because it reflects the choices we make every day. We tend to do a good job putting ourselves together on days with important meetings or presentations, but remember: presence is 24/7. Some professionals find it hard to make good choices on "regular" days, when working from home, or in a business casual environment. Here are some tips and reminders:

➲ Consider the position you have and the position you want. Dress one notch above what is expected for your current position.

➲ Pay attention to details. Before going in to the office, check the heels and soles of your shoes. Are they scuffed? Get a shine. Are they worn? Then replace them. Shirts should always be pressed, especially when working from home. Worn or frayed hems should always be repaired. Buy a full-length mirror and do a head-to-toe check every day, front and back.

➲ Fit is it! Clothes should never be too tight. If you are a hard-to-fit person, consider buying "up" a size and tailoring down to fit. You must be able to button a suit jacket or sports jacket. Sleeves and pants should never be too long or too short. Find a good tailor even for your "business casual" clothing.

➲ Get a good haircut. Men, keep the back of your neck neat and clean. Women, keep your hair out of your face so that we can see your eyes, and spray it so you don't have to flip it or arrange it during the day.

⊃ Flip-flops and casual sandals are acceptable if you work at the beach; otherwise, wear appropriate footwear whenever you are inside the building. Consider keeping a spare pair of dressier shoes (plus socks or hose) in the office just in case.

⊃ Business casual clothing should reflect your industry and company. "Artistic" is fine if that is your field. "Traditional" and conservative are more appropriate for most financial services companies.

⊃ Never "dress down" on days when you're expecting out-of-town clients, interviewing others, or meeting with government agencies.

⊃ Be aware of creating excess noise during meetings, presentations, or conference calls. Women, be sure your jewelry is not jingling, and men be aware of jangling the keys or change in your pocket.

⊃ Be light with perfume or aftershave. Too much fragrance in an enclosed space not only gives people a headache, but it can create a second story about you and your confidence level.

⊃ You need to feel great every day when you get dressed for work, even when working remotely. If something is bothering you about the way you look, fix it.

⊃ When you are onsite, always check the local or departmental guidelines for acceptable work attire, either in your normal location or in a locale where you are visiting for work purposes.

➲ You don't need to spend a lot of money to look good at work. Consider a wardrobe of fewer, but better, pieces. Maintain it by adding one or two new pieces each season and rotating out pieces that are more than five years old.

➲ Finally, you look good when you feel good. Exercise and nutrition make a big difference in one's energy level. Yes, there's the added bonus of looking a little better in our clothes, but there's also the spring in our step and the shine in our eyes that tell others we are engaged and alive.[26]

Remember, the people who see you every day are the ones who make decisions about your future.

What Else Do They See?

Your PowerPoint slides and printed handouts are also a factor of "look" and thus a part of your brand. Overly dense slides in particular can detract from one's presence and suggest different descriptive words, like "vague," "disorganized," and even "overwhelmed." Be sure your brand carries through all of your written materials and slides.

We must manage all aspects of our "look." Even the appearance of your office or work space tells people what to think and say about you. Remember Delia from Chapter Five? The condition of her office was a negative data point in the way she was viewed by senior management. Your office/work space says a great deal about who you are and how you see yourself. Everything from the way your work materials are arranged to the pile of untouched journals in your in-box to the artwork on the walls and books on the shelves of your home office: all of these are data points.

Here are two examples:

I was once asked to coach a very smart but somewhat shy woman we'll call Dayna. Her boss was a big fan of hers; he felt she had a lot to offer and wanted her to display a more confident image and presence. When I went to Dayna's office for our first meeting, I looked at her extremely clean desk and tabletop and the sparse items on the shelves, and I asked her if she had just moved in to the office. "No," she said. "I've been here for eight years."

Hmm, I wondered. Maybe it is possible to wear an "invisibility cloak" at work. When I visit new coaching clients for the first time, I get a lot of clues from their physical environment. Dayna made no imprint on that office, which I saw as representative of the larger presence challenge her boss wanted us to address. Dayna admitted that in meetings, she preferred to listen rather than speak, and so again we have a case of making no imprint on the topic being discussed. Based on the data points she was (or wasn't) putting out there, Dayna was a little bit like the wallpaper: it's there, but we rarely notice it after awhile. **The absence of obvious data points is still data**: *even a whole lotta nothing says something.*

◆

Lillian and her husband both worked for the same company for more than ten years. Although they were in different divisions, he was a big wheel and everyone knew she was his wife. After a painful and very visible divorce, Lillian decided to accept a new job in a different company where she could be known as something other than "the former Mrs. X." Lillian was very deliberate about the kind of impression she wanted to create at her new company. When she brought some personal items to decorate her new office, she chose things that would help her create her new brand and stimulate positive conversations. For instance, she is a runner and a sailing enthusiast, so she filled her credenza with snapshots from races and regattas. On the wall she has a signed framed photo of a famous runner, and her smart-looking gym bag is usually sitting next to her desk. As her brand of "active and athletic" became known, people started to mention different events to her, including a 5K run that the company sponsored.

Lillian also saw herself as a bright and optimistic person, and so every week she treated herself to fresh flowers that she happily bought from the flower stand at the train station, choosing the brightest blooms she could find. People began stopping by on Mondays just to see this week's flowers, engaging in a little small talk, and even bringing up light news from around the department. This helped Lillian and her coworkers get to know each other better. Finally, Lillian was deliberate about what she did not put in her office. She did not bring in any family vacation photos because she didn't want to answer questions about her husband, and she wasn't ready to talk about the complicated custody arrangements they had regarding the children. Best to leave that for later, when she felt stronger and had built some trust with her colleagues.

Dayna missed some opportunities to let people know who she was and what she stood for. She was an amazing woman with a truly unique background, but she had no clue how to let that shine in the often uptight corporate world. Together, we chose some ways that helped her express her individuality through her office décor and how she dressed. For instance, she loved modern art, so she brought in some colorful, vibrant prints that really popped on the plain white walls of her office. She also started to wear multihued geometric scarves and more interesting jewelry. Dayna made new choices so she could shed her cloak of invisibility. Like Lillian, she wanted to be deliberate and thoughtful in creating her personal brand.

Rebuilding Your Brand

By now I hope it has become clear to you how important it is to be purposeful and attentive in creating your brand. Remember, every interaction is a data point, and every moment needs to be managed in order create and/or strengthen your brand. A good brand will support you through the occasional "moment of regret" as we learned in Chapter One, and you read about several techniques to help you avoid or recover from such moments. But suppose this information has come a little too late for you? Suppose you've created multiple "negative" data points and the buzz about you is not so good right now? Maybe that's the reason you bought this book.

If you are in a reputational hole, is it possible to dig out and rebuild your brand?

"Yes, it is possible," says Davia Temin, reputational expert and columnist for *Forbes*. "Maybe you won't be able to return 100 percent to your previous state, but it is possible to get out of that hole and create something new." I love this idea, because once again it gives you the choice. "In fact," added Temin, "It's not *if* you will or will not rebuild your reputation, it's *how* you will rebuild it."[27]

How, indeed?

1. "First, you need to understand—deeply understand— what got you into the hole to begin with," says Temin. I agree. As we discussed in Chapter Three, you need to identify your triggers and stay ahead of them. Perhaps the pressure of something at work caused you to snap at people; perhaps the stress of long hours or extra travel caused you to behave unthinkingly toward your staff. Whatever it was, you need to own your behavior as well as the impact it had. Apologize, and set about fixing it. Strong brands such as Toyota and Tylenol were able to weather some pretty challenging times because they stood behind their products, owned the problem, promised to fix it, fixed it, and won people's trust again.

2. You need to decide how you want to be known now. As Temin says: "The world moves on. You will never be the same person, but luckily, the world is never the same either." Think about it: people and projects come and go. Take a look at your new world and decide how you want to be known now, and go through the aspirational adjectives exercise with the new wisdom gained from this difficult experience. But whatever adjective you choose, remember, it had better be true.

3. You need to assess your environment in order to determine if "they" will allow you to reinvent yourself. Will your colleagues be willing to trust you again? Are you willing

to do what it takes to earn that trust? If so, take heart in that. "Public figures reinvent themselves all the time," says Temin, "and in America we like people who can bounce back from adversity. Look at Bill Clinton."

4. Finally, you need to believe in yourself. People will take their cues from you, and they will be watching you carefully. If you keep your camera off during most videoconferences, or if you walk around with your head down and your shoulders bowed, you will not be demonstrating your own confidence in your abilities, and you will not show that you were, and will be, a successful leader. Go back and review your strengths from Chapter Three. Remind yourself of the powerful, positive aspects of your presence and bring those to the forefront once again.

To sum up, whether you are strengthening a vibrant positive brand or rebuilding a wilted one, it all goes back to what we said in Chapter One: it takes mindfulness, not magic, to create enough data points so people can connect the dots in the way that you want them to be connected. To do so, you need to be deliberate and focused in every interaction, clear on your purpose, supremely other-focused, and aligned in word and deed—in other words, fully present.

MOMENT TO
REFLECT

- ❑ People are already talking about you. Being deliberate about your brand helps them know what to say about you.

- ❑ The belief that "a good job speaks for itself" is outdated and naïve.

- ❑ Strong brands offer protection in good times and in bad.

- ❑ To establish your brand, you have to "tell 'em and show 'em" many times.

- ❑ Physical appearance is an important part of your brand.

- ❑ It is possible to correct misperceptions people have about you by rebranding yourself.

7

PUTTING IT ALL TOGETHER

Jean-Paul is the CEO of a small but prestigious manufacturing company in the rural part of a northeastern state. A former Wall Street power broker, he left "the craziness" in favor of a slower, more family-friendly environment. He's an extremely likable, gregarious guy who listens intently and makes excellent eye contact. In fact, the way that he listens makes one feel important. He's also a fellow who knows who he is and what he stands for. As Jean-Paul talks about his work, his colleagues, and his family, you can hear the foundation of his core values shining subtly through every sentence. If you met him in a coffee shop on a day when he was not dressed in a corporate power suit, you'd find him comfortably attired in a denim shirt and khaki trousers, casual, and yet beautifully pressed and well-tailored.

Jean-Paul's company has the license for a particular type of technology that is essential to other manufacturers in the United States, and while they have some competitors, no one delivers with the quality that their company does. Their commitment to quality was one of the reasons Jean-Paul chose this job offer over others at larger companies, and under his leadership this little company has become a recognized presence in its niche marketplace. It is not surprising that Jean-Paul's company has been approached recently regarding potential mergers or acquisition. The senior leadership team has its work cut out for it as it considers numerous potential deals and offers. Jean-Paul has made one thing crystal clear: the company will strike no deal unless all of the employees who worked to build the company can benefit substantially from the sale or merger of the company, not just the management team but the folks in the lab and the ones on the shop floor too.

◆

You've met many leaders in the book who represent the entire spectrum of presence strengths and development opportunities. I saved the story of Jean-Paul for this chapter because he embodies the center of the presence model where everything comes together. Let's take a look.

Heads Up's Presence Model

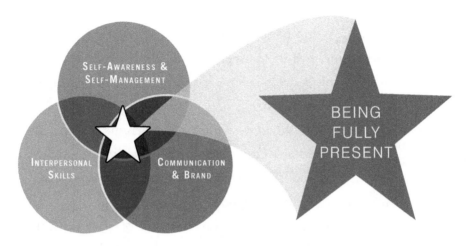

Now that we've reached the center of the presence model, let's first remind ourselves of the three circles and explore why the center is devoted to "being fully present" and supporting leadership behaviors.

I.   Self-Awareness and Self-Management

Self-management comes from self-awareness. When we are truly self-aware and able to put self-consciousness aside, we can be fully present with others. Leaders who are cited as having excellent presence always demonstrate strong self-awareness. They are clear on their strengths and weaknesses, and they are also very clear on who they are and what they stand for, like Jean-Paul. Noted author and emotional intelligence expert Daniel Goleman said, "We lead ourselves before we ever lead others, and how we lead ourselves depends on how well we know ourselves."[28]

II.　Interpersonal Skills

Presence is only presence if you are with someone. Being fully present means it is almost always "all about them." Yes, there is a dynamic between being self-aware and being other-aware, but fundamentally being present means being there, really there, for them. When we are in another person's presence, we honor that person by being supremely other-focused, attuned emotionally, and listening actively, like Jean-Paul. When those behaviors are returned, rapport can grow and, eventually, so can trust. Most of the leadership team was in place when Jean-Paul was hired to be CEO, and yet his 360° feedback shows that he quickly gained their trust and respect. Leaders who are other-focused instead of self-focused are seen as good stewards of the organization. The whole leader-as-servant movement is essentially about this idea.[29] We are tired of selfish, conniving leaders who run our companies and our 401k plans into the ground. When we see a pattern of positive behavior where the leader puts the company and its welfare first, we believe in that leader and accept her leadership as well as her partnership.

III.　Communication and Brand

Every time you communicate, it is your presence in action. When you take the time to find out who your communication partners are and what they want or need from you, and when you create your communiqué with them in mind, you are respecting your audience and demonstrating that you value the relationship. In communication, being fully present means you are deeply other-conscious during the preparation and the delivery of your message, and intensely focused on the verbal and nonverbal responses of your audience.

The Center of the Presence Model

Being Fully Present:

- ➲ Being in the Moment

- ➲ Giving others our full attention

- ➲ Sharing personal experience to demonstrate understanding

- ➲ Encouraging interaction and collaboration

- ➲ Demonstrating empathy and compassion

Being in the Moment

We've spent a great deal of time in this book learning how to manage the moments, but perhaps the best way to manage them is to stay really present in them. It's so easy to get distracted these days between the Smartphone, the Blackberry, and IM, and there's no time to think between e-mails, phone calls, and back-to-back meetings. Sound familiar? These conditions foster the opposite of mindfulness. In the jumble of thoughts and information, we sometimes find ourselves in a state of mindlessness. We are a little bit "lost in space." But "Danger, Will Robinson!"[30] In this state we are not fully present. The danger is that, like Alec in Chapter Four, potential pitfalls are lurking, and in our mindless state we miss the warning signals. When we can stay in the moment, we can pick up spoken and unspoken clues and respond in a thoughtful and timely fashion.

PREMISE #9

*Being in the Moment Allows Us to Adapt Quickly
and to Actively Influence What Happens Next*

In their excellent *HBR* article "Leadership in a (Permanent) Crisis," authors Heifetz, Grashow, and Linsky talk about the "hunker-down" mentality of some leaders and managers during and after the 2008–2009 recession. Taken literally, hunkering down means assuming a crouched, defensive position. When people are afraid of getting hit by something or someone, they will likely "duck and cover." In the business world, hunkering down means hiding from a difficult situation or assuming a defensive posture in order to avoid a potentially threatening outcome. For example, people will hesitate to suggest new or novel approaches. They will avoid saying or doing anything to "rock the boat" or appear extraneous. I felt it in my business during that time. People were hesitant to sign up for our two-day seminars because they didn't want anyone to make the leap that if they could be gone from their desk for two days, maybe they weren't really "mission critical" after all. This is a very natural response to the threat, real or imagined, of losing one's job in a bad economy. However, for leaders, there needs to be a different response.

Heifetz, Grashow, and Linsky believe that leaders who practice the opposite of hunkering down—what they call "adaptive leadership"—are much more able to ride out turbulent times and help themselves and others adapt successfully to the new normal. "In this context," they say, "leadership is an improvisational and experimental art."[31] I love this phrase. Why? Because it has everything to do with presence:

⮑ Let's start with "improvisational": Anyone who has taken a theater course or been in a play has likely participated in improvisational exercises. These are completely unscripted interactions in which the actors build on what they are given by their fellow actors in that moment. Brilliant comic actors and writers, such as Tina Fey and Ana Gasteyter, come out of the improv tradition. In fact, in her very funny autobiography *Bossypants*, Fey shares the basic "rules for improv," which might seem a bit oxymoronic, but which are essential to hold the skit together. These rules also make very good sense for leaders looking to engage others and foster collaboration and creativity, because while we aren't exactly appearing on *Saturday Night Live*, we are in a continuous, long-running, live performance and it helps to know the rules. And the rule is the same whether you are a business leader or an actor: success in a facile, unscripted environment demands that you *be present*, totally in the moment, focused 100 percent on what is happening in front of you.

➲ Heifetz, Grashow, and Linksy also said that in turbulent times leadership is an "experimental art." I'm guessing that the word "experimental" is making a few readers cringe right now (and maybe the word "art" is too), so let's break it down. You'll find lots of research-based articles about the science of leadership, and indeed, we have many ways to scientifically measure a leader's effectiveness, everything from 360° assessments to productivity analyses. Leadership is both an art and a science. Productivity measurement is an example of the science. What is the art? The art is the creative side of leadership, the part that is created with our minds, hearts, and imaginations, and like every art form, the art of good leadership becomes more valuable with time and practice. Experimental artists are out in front; thus they are leaders too. Think about the first abstract painters and modern dancers. They had a vision of what their art could be and they were willing to consider new approaches. In fact, they were driven to try something new, and as initiators of anything brand new, they were likely met with pretty strong reactions from critics and public alike. Hmm, not too dissimilar from how we feel as business leaders sometimes.

There are more similarities. In fact, as leaders in organizations, you play two roles: On one hand you are the experimental artist, frustrated or disillusioned with the old way of doing things, and wanting to try something new. On the other hand, as a manager or decision maker, you are also the producer or benefactor, the person who enables artists to try something new, knowing they have the support of their sponsor. As the artist, how does it feel to come up with a new idea and hear "Yes"? Pretty amazing. But here's the thing: as the sponsor, it feels fantastic to be able to say, "Yes, let's try that." This is the opposite of hunkering down. This is the act of opening up, of expanding, of brainstorming. And how do we do that in the moment? Here is where the rules of improv come in again. Tina Fey says another rule[32] is to follow your conversation partner's offering with "Yes … and," which expands on the idea your partner has introduced.

"Yes…and" means "I want to explore this with you." It means, "This is an idea worth building on … let's do that now!" It is not duck and cover, looking for the flaw, threat or potential pitfall—not right now. It is simply a way of opening up the dialogue; we can evaluate or critique later.

Yes…and: Think about the power this phrase would have in our everyday work conversations in which we are looking to build, solve, or create. What might that sound like in our world?

> **Example:** A colleague says to the leader: "I think we need to do something fresh for the teambuilding segment of managers' retreat in the spring. The reviews from last year's 'cross the swamp' game were dismal. So I was thinking, what if we put people in teams and have them do something practical, like build shelves for the community center or make a meal for a soup kitchen?"

Scenario A: The leader says, "Well, then we'd have to have a lot of tools, or stoves, or something like that and we'd have to worry about people getting cut or burned…"

Scenario B: The leader says, "Yes, I like the idea of something practical, but what would we do about all the tools and stoves and food…"

Scenario C: The leader says, "Yes, I like the idea of something practical, *and* if we can tie it to one of our charitable causes, that would be a win-win." Colleague: "Oh, I've got it! Our CEO just made a speech about Big Brothers Big Sisters. What if we had the teams build bicycles for the kids?"

Clearly, the leader in Scenario A is not coming into the conversation with an open and experimental attitude. Talk about dismal! That hunker-down response would certainly squash the creative dialogue. The leader in Scenario B starts out with "yes" and then goes into hunker-down mode, signaled by the dreaded word "but." "But" is the word that negates everything that comes before it and makes it really difficult to keep the interaction moving forward in a creative way. In Scenario C, the leader is looking to build on the good idea introduced by the colleague. Can't you just imagine how the rest of that dialogue went? Whatever the exact words, the dialog itself was likely quite positive, engaging, and productive. This leader knows that this dialogue is in its earliest and thus most creative stage. Perhaps this leader also believes that when the team comes up with the ideal solution, they will also ensure that things happen safely. The leader doesn't need to get in the way of the process right now; she can check in later if need be. Scenario C is so much better. You knew it when you saw it. The question is: Can you think and speak like that with your team?

Finally, here's one more very important reason to consider "experimental" approaches: The old rules and norms no longer apply in periods of intense change and reconfiguring. As "adaptive leaders" you and your colleagues need to live in the present in order to figure out what works *now*. You need to determine how people are feeling *now* and what they need from you to stay productive and focused *now*. You have the overall vision, and you have the strategic mindset that will keep things moving forward, but the decisions and tasks to get to that future are happening today.

Over the years I have coached many high-achieving type-A professionals, and I've noticed that extremely goal-oriented people  always seem to live in the future, at least in their imaginations. They envision a utopia where all their goals are achieved, not just their personal goals, but their team's goals and their company's goals, and that idea is so compelling to them that they can't wait to get there. Their mission is goal achievement. One executive coach I know calls these people "achievement junkies" and for them, today's tasks are just chores or even obstacles getting in the way of their next fix. They are often impatient with these tasks and the people doing the tasks. There are two problems with this:

1. They are rewarded for goal achievement and so feel justified in their quest, and thus they see their impatience (and often, their subsequent rudeness or coldness) as simply a

means to an end. This is not okay, as we saw in the case of Robert, our supply chain manager in Chapter Four.

2. Single-minded goal achievement is like putting blinders on a thoroughbred, leading it to the track, and firing the starting pistol. As long as the horse stays on the track, it will definitely cross the finish line with some decent speed, no problem. However, the world of work today is anything but linear: There is no track, and sometimes there isn't even a finish line. How can that be? Because the world is always moving on: The technology we had when we envisioned the solution two years ago is different now; the team members we had when we formed the task force six months ago are different now; leaders change, markets change, laws and regulations change, competitors change, and we are often figuring out both the track and the end goal as we go along. It's improv all day long.

I understand the dynamic tension between the future and the present: you are being held accountable for achieving the goal. It affects your results, your review, and maybe even your reputation. But once again, it's not just *what* you achieve; it's *how* you achieve it. Whenever you feel yourself growing dangerously impatient because it feels as if "they" aren't getting to the finish line fast enough, stop, breathe, think, and then act. Don't yell, don't rip the phone out of the wall, and don't roll your eyes or put someone down. Do find the ways to convey openness, creativity, and collaboration because there are people on your staff right now who are ready to create new, workable solutions to your team's challenges. Are you open to their ideas? Can you take the blinders off and experiment a bit? They might have an idea that would get you to the goal sooner or, even better, create a superior goal. And through this whole process, can you be *100 percent present* for them whenever you are with them?

Please write a positive intention (see box below) for yourself regarding being fully present.

_____

_____

_____

Positive Intentions

A positive intention is when you have an intention to change something and you phrase it in a positive way.

- *An intention: Stop interrupting people.*

- *A positive intention: Listen patiently until my conversational partner is finished.*

- *An intention: Stop procrastinating.*

- *A positive intention: Start early.*

Positive intentions work better because they work with the way our brains are wired. For instance, by thinking "stop interrupting," I merely embed the word "interrupt" more deeply in my brain. By saying "listen patiently" to myself, I embed those two words in my brain. If I do so consistently, I can replace my old bad habit with my desired intention in just a few weeks.

Giving Others Our Full Attention

Suppose you are talking on the phone. Can you tell when the other person isn't really paying attention? Of course you can, most of the time. (And you definitely can when you hear the click of the other person's keyboard or—true story—the sound of *Angry Birds* in the background.) So if it's obvious to us when others are doing it, can we deduce that it's obvious to them when we are doing it? Of course we can.

When you feel your attention wandering, do you know why? What routinely gets in the way of giving others your full attention?

_____

_____

_____

You probably listed some of the things mentioned earlier, like IM and other interrupters. Did you also list some of your own personal attention grabbers? These could be anything from the view outside your office door (i.e., you can see who is going in and out of your boss's office) to the wailing sirens from the fire station down the street. Here's one of mine: When I am seeing many coaching clients in a day, I find it hard to give people my full attention if I am physically uncomfortable. If the room is too hot or if I am hungry or tired, I find my attention wavering even though I am trained to pay attention for long periods of time. I know this about myself, and so I make sure that I dress in layers, and I plan rest breaks in between clients so I can stay energized all day.

ACTIVITY

What steps might you take to be able to give others your full attention? Please write these as positive intentions:

_____

_____

_____

Sharing Personal Experience to Demonstrate Understanding

You may notice that as you become more and more attuned to others, you'll find yourself empathizing with them. You might even remember a time in your career when you faced the same or a similar challenge. Consider sharing your story with your colleague. It's comforting to people to hear that they aren't the only ones who struggled with something, and it's inspiring to know that even their leader overcame challenges in earlier days. Here's an example from Nelson, division president for a financial services company, speaking with a young salesperson:

> *"I do understand what you're going through. When I was a new salesperson, I had a lot of difficulty asking for the sale. I could present product features and build rapport with the best of them, but when it came time to close, I just froze up. At one time, my closing ratio was the lowest in the country. I knew I had to figure out how to fix it, so I spent some time with the two senior salespeople in my regional office and had them walk me through, word for word, exactly how they closed their last three or four sales. As they talked me through it, I realized it was actually pretty simple. The only obstacle was in my head. It was a good lesson. So, how can I help you today?"*

We've probably all met "Nelsons" in our careers who motivated us to persevere. Their generosity in sharing their stories with us is inspirational. There is an art and a science to sharing personal stories. Notice how Nelson began his story: he first expressed empathy, and then he chose a story that was relevant to the challenge his younger colleague was facing. Nelson was artful in sharing this story. His underlying message was: "You may struggle early in your career but it won't kill your career; I'm an example of that." Notice that Nelson's story is brief and still complete: He gave the background, the steps he took, what he learned, and offered support—all in less than a minute. That's the science. In sharing personal stories there is a temptation to overshare. If we share too much personal information, the focus of the story becomes about us and not about them. While the story is technically from our own experience, it is intended to help them. They need to readily see the parallels between their own situation and the story we are telling. If we overtalk or overshare, that intention is lost.

Encouraging Interaction and Collaboration

One of the VPs that I coach has a larger-than-life presence. She has a strong intellect matched by verbal acuity, an outgoing personality, and a quick wit. When she is physically in a room, other people naturally look to her for leadership and guidance. She's working on strengthening the leadership team directly below her on the organizational chart. One of her strategies is to get team members to interact and collaborate more so that they don't always depend on her for ideas or for tacit approval. I noticed when I observed her with her team members that even when she tries to hold back to let them run the discussion, they constantly check her face for signs of approval or disapproval when new ideas come up. I applaud her because she is self-aware and courageous enough to realize that from time to time she needs to physically remove herself from some meetings so that the team will create its own dynamic.

If you are the leader (by position, subject-matter expertise, personality, or other) it can't be all about you if you want your team members to build relationships with each other. Remember that just by virtue of your position you have a big presence in the room or on the call. You have to manage this. Of course, the degree to which the leader can "step out" depends on the team members' experience and appetite for independence, but if you want to demonstrate that you are ready for the next level, you have to give them a chance to show that they are too.

Here are three tips for encouraging interaction on your team:

1. Be overt regarding your expectations. Tell team members specifically what you mean by collaboration, how you expect them to collaborate, and why you think it is so important for them and for you. Acknowledge it whenever you notice people collaborating.

2. Use open-ended questions that encourage team members to talk to each other in meetings, and listen both actively and patiently. In other words, stay in the moment, but resist the temptation to jump in and take over. Use your position of power to ask team members to respond to their colleagues' statements. Use nonverbals to acknowledge people whenever they participate. Remember, you are the role model for listening and acknowledging.

3. Make connections between people. They may not be able to see the big picture the way that you can from your level, and so they may not readily see that there is an opportunity for cooperation or collaboration. Don't assume they are just being resistant (though some may be); make the introduction and offer some ideas as to how collaboration might work.

If you do all three of these things, your team will quickly learn what you expect and will start making the effort to work together.

Demonstrating Empathy and Compassion

At this point in the book we've talked many times about the fact that we bring our feelings with us to work, whether we want to or not. The behavior of demonstrating empathy and compassion is in the center of the presence model because it requires healthy doses of other-awareness, self-awareness and self-management, plus strong listening skills. Let's explore.

First, what do these words mean? If you check a dictionary definition, *empathy* is "the intellectual understanding of how another person feels." The words "empathy" and "sympathy" are often used interchangeably, although sympathy is defined more as a "sharing of feelings." In other words, empathy is "I know what you're feeling" and sympathy is "I feel what you're feeling." *Compassion* is a shared feeling of deep sympathy accompanied by a strong desire to alleviate the suffering of the other. In a business setting, our compassion is aroused when we are attuned to another person's feelings and we sense that person is struggling or unhappy. For instance, if you see someone on your team really wrestling with a challenge, as Nelson did, and you feel compelled to step in to offer direction, advice or encouragement, it's not just because it's your job; it's because your sense of compassion was aroused.

For our compassion to be aroused, we must be fully present and attuned to detect emotions in others. We might be reading people's body language at a meeting or presentation or listening to their voices during a phone call, but when we are fully present we pick up both the spoken and unspoken messages. Picking up these clues means getting out of your head and into the room. Some clients (usually men) tell me that they just aren't good at this. Phooey! There's no get-out-of-jail-free card for women or men on this one. Detecting emotion through subtext is a skill that can be developed or strengthened by almost anyone. In fact, Daniel Goleman says that while the data show women are better at detecting another person's fleeting feelings, as shown in the face, men are just as good at picking up "emotional leakage" from other forms of body language, including tone of voice, and especially at work where people often try to mask their true emotions by controlling their facial expressions.[33]

Detecting emotions is the first step. Responding to those emotions with empathy and compassion is the second step. Interestingly, gender does play a part in how we respond, not because women or men are better at responding, but because of people's stereotypical expectations regarding empathetic responses from men or women. Goleman states the unattractive but obvious truth: people don't expect men to demonstrate empathy. Yet, based on his review of the data, Goleman surmised that men have as much latent ability for empathy as women, but often have less motivation to express that empathy.[34] Catalyst took this question even further in a fascinating report published in 2005.[35] While the organization's review of more

than forty different studies showed very little difference between women's and men's actual leadership *behavior*, people's *perceptions* about a leader's effectiveness could be skewed, depending on the leader's gender. Overall, Catalyst found that in spite of women's actual behavior, there were misleading *perceptions* that women are better at taking care, while men are better at taking charge. So it is expected that women will express empathy and compassion, and when they don't, it is jarring to others (as we saw with Bettina in Chapter Four). Likewise, when men do express empathy, they are given extra credit because it's simply not expected. Remember, people have expectations based on context, fair or unfair, and gender is as much a part of context as is one's role and level.

While we must be present to attune to others and respond appropriately, demonstrating compassion actually affects presence as well because it helps us stay calm, focused, and mindful. How? Neuroscience explains that demonstrating compassion engages the parasympathetic nervous system, which increases the body's natural healing power. Richard Boyatzis[36] and his colleagues at Case Western Reserve published research showing that leaders who coach others with compassion actually experience a reduction in their stress level and show healing in the areas of the body damaged by stress. Let's take a moment and be clear on the difference between managing and coaching: Managing is about getting things done through others; coaching is a helping behavior, intended to aid others in their quest for growth or improvement. Jake, our big-box retail manager from Chapter One told me that when he needs "a little bit of feel good" he goes out on the floor for an hour to coach or train some of the associates; not to look at inventory levels or supervise the front end of the store, but to coach and mentor. He always describes those days as good days. So, go ahead. **Coach with compassion. It's good for you.**

The second reason to demonstrate compassion is to build productive, lasting relationships at work. Expressions of empathy or compassion tell others that we care about them as people, and not just as workers. Remember the reasons why people chose certain leaders for the Leaders with Presence list in Chapter One? Right. Many times it was because the leader demonstrated a little humanity, and expressed interest in the other person as a person. By demonstrating empathy and compassion, we are engaging others on a deeper level and fostering stronger bonds. We are connecting to people in ways they remember for a long time.

Ah, but there are other things people remember for a long time. Jessica, Mark, Bettina, Alec, and other leaders profiled in this book found out the hard way that the accumulation of stress can trigger an unwelcome and unproductive reaction, and the severity or drama of that reaction can become the stuff of legends.

PREMISE #10:

Stress Is the Poison of Presence

Remember the saber-tooth tiger in Chapter Two? That tiger represents the person or situation that triggers a strong emotional response in each of us. You did some work to identify your own triggers and create a plan for staying ahead of them when you can, and recovering from them when you can't. Now we want to show you how these stressors or triggers impact your presence so you know what behaviors to manage when you are under stress. Consider these examples:

My client Ray and I were practicing the Q&A portion of his upcoming presentation, and I asked him a controversial question. He lost his fragile composure and with a deep frown on his face he snapped, "That question doesn't belong in this meeting!" Then he stopped himself, suddenly realizing how he must have come across. "I didn't feel that coming," he said. "What do I do if that happens again?"

◆

Corrinne was shocked when we watched the video of her telling a particularly emotional story in which one of her direct reports made her angry. "Oh my gosh!" she said. "Look at what I'm doing with my face! Look at what I'm doing with my hands!" Without any prompting from me, Corrinne noticed that her upper lip was curling such that her eyeteeth were showing, like a snarl, and she was making abrupt "chopping" motions with her hands. I brought her attention to how shrill her voice became when she was stressed by having her close her eyes and listen to the recording at the start of our interview, when she was calm, and then again at the peak point in the story. She said, "I sound like the Wicked Witch. I had no idea I was doing those things."

◆

Stress is the poison of presence. It erodes our ability to manage those moments when we most need to be present and show presence.

What shows up for you when you are stressed? And how do you know? Are you one of those people who suffer from tunnel vision or self-blindness when stressed? How can you find out what you're putting out there? Maybe you already have some idea: perhaps you've gotten feedback or coaching from someone close to you, or you've noticed people's reactions when you express yourself more stridently than you planned. I once had someone say to me on the phone, "There's no need to raise your voice," when I didn't realize my frustration was showing quite that much. I remember that period of time as one of high pressure on the whole department. We were walking around in a constant state of stress. Looking back on that situation with the clarity that comes with time and distance, I recall that the person on the phone was telling me that my request didn't follow the rules, which struck me as rigid, inflexible, and unhelpful. I couldn't actually say that to her, of course, but in a way I did say it—through my tone of voice. And I didn't know it.

Often people sign up for our presence seminars because they want to increase their self-awareness and manage some aspect of their presence that manifests itself under stress. The table below includes the Essential Elements of Communication from Chapter Five, plus the behaviors that show up when we are being present. The column of the left gives behavioral examples of the impact stress might have on each element. The column on the right shows more ideal behavior, such as what would display in a relaxed state.

Leader's Presence Assessment		
STRESSED ↓		RELAXED ↓
Essential Elements—Look		
Looks down, away; keeps camera off, avoids looking at camera	Eye Contact	Direct, expressive
Worried, angry, grim; flat affect	Facial Expression	Animated; smiles; genuine
Hunched shoulders, makes fists; crossed arms tight to body; choppy or no gestures	Shoulders, hands, arms	Relaxed, loose, appropriate gestures
Slumped	Posture	Straight without being stiff; shoulders back
Pacing, fidgeting	Unconscious/habitual movements	Calm body; hand stillness
Ill-fitting, wrinkled, sloppy	Clothing, makeup, jewelry	Effortlessly professional top to toe
Messy, wordy, overdone, off the point	Handouts, slides, reports	Attractive, clean design enhances the speaker and message
Essential Elements—Sound		
Staccato and rushed OR sluggish and tired	Speed of speech	Calm, slow enough to allow for full expression but fast enough to generate energy
Does not pause, OR pauses mid-phrase or mid-sentence	Use of pauses	Well placed, well timed; natural
Too loud or too soft	Volume	Appropriate for the space and message
Monotone and dull OR sharp edgy tones that grate	Tonality	Melody supports message; easy to listen to
Sloppy articulation; insufficient breath to support the voice; too fast	Pronunciation or accent	Takes time to fully articulate each word
Increased unconscious use of filler	Filler	Manages delivery, pace and breath to eliminate filler; uses studied breath

Continued on following page...

Leader's Presence Assessment		
STRESSED		RELAXED
Essential Elements—Content		
Wanders from main point; disjointed	Organization & Flow	Well structured; flows cleanly; makes sense
Too much detail; overtalks; overanswers questions	Focus & Brevity	Stays within time limits while hitting main points
No clear purpose; audience unsure why they are getting this message	Clarity of purpose	Speaker is clear on purpose and the approach to get there
Part or all of key message is missing or blurred by extraneous detail.	Key message apparent	Main concept, action, and result are clear to the audience (what, how, why)
Unsure or unclear POV	Point of view	Has POV and is prepared to share it
Sentences run together with "and, and," or "so, so."	Run-on speech	Sentences end cleanly with a clear pause and breath.
Aimed at too high or too low a level	Relevant to audience	Message resonates with audience because created with them in mind.
Used thoughtlessly, thus disconnects from a mixed audience	Jargon	Used specifically to connect to a homogenous audience
Being Fully Present		
Easily distracted; interrupts; listens without hearing; looks away	Giving others full attention	Maintains eye contact; minimizes interruptions
Hogs the floor; plays the blame game	Encouraging interaction & collaboration	Uses questions to engage others; facilitates rather than directs
Abrupt, all-business; does not notice or accommodate others' emotional needs	Demonstrating empathy & compassion	Shows warmth and understanding; asks about person's nonwork life
No positive affect; disconnected from the mission; overly focused on tasks versus people	Generating enthusiasm in others	Shares optimism; engages positive emotion in self and others
"Coporate speak"; generic messages void of meaning	Sharing personal experiences	Uses stories from own experience; connects to others' situation
No emotional expression; appears to be pretending	Leveraging own emotions to connect with others	Acknowledges own and others' feelings in an open manner

The "relaxed" behaviors in the right column are what we are aiming for, either because we truly *are* relaxed on the inside or we want to manage our behavior on the outside until the inside catches up (or slows down as the case may be.)

Since the behaviors on the left show up when people are anxious, upset, or triggered, these are the warning signals that you should pay attention to in order to analyze the source of your stress and take steps to get ahead of it. Remember, these behaviors show up as audible or visible clues to other people who will connect the dots in any way that makes sense to them. *Moreover, the behaviors on the left side can be interpreted as a stress response even when you may not be stressed, nervous, or anxious.* As we said all the way back in Chapter Three, you can't manage what you don't know. Do what you need to do to be sure you understand what data points you put out there when you're feeling good—and when you're not.

Stand in the Center

The center of the presence model is where everything comes together, and you can stand in the center, like Jean-Paul. When you consciously manage the moments—as many as you can—you move closer to your goal of being a great leader, and you dramatically increase the likelihood that you will end up on someone's Leaders with Presence list.

The leader you admire could be you.

MOMENT TO
REFLECT

❑ Success in a facile, unscripted environment demands that we focus on what is happening right here, right now. The best way to manage any moment is to stay really present in that moment, fully aware of what is occurring and ready to respond appropriately.

❑ Positive intentions help us articulate changes we want to make, worded in such a way that they help us form new habits instead of trying to break old, entrenched habits.

❑ Good leaders are able to share personal stories to motivate and inspire others.

❑ To detect emotions and respond with compassion, one must be fully present. Expressing compassion affects presence because it decreases the negative impacts of stress.

❑ Stress is the poison of presence. It impacts our behavior, and thus our presence, in very specific ways.

8

DEVELOPING YOUR SIGNATURE PRESENCE

What's *Your* Story?

Each chapter of this book starts with a story based on real leaders in business today. Through these stories we hope you recognized a bit of yourself or someone else whose presence is a work in progress. We hope you found comfort in the fact that your struggles are not unique. No one is born with perfect presence, even those leaders who seem to have it all together. Every conscientious leader I know, regardless of level, is working on being a better boss, communicator, and leader.

We talked a bit in Chapter Two about the stereotypical expectations people make because of someone's role or level. There's a larger, more pervasive stereotype out there: the corporate drone. Just this week on a popular sitcom about a group of nerdy guys, the lead characters were desperately trying to find a way to fund their pet project because if they couldn't get funding, they'd "have to become corporate drones." It got a big laugh. At one point in my professional career, I wouldn't have thought it was funny. In fact, it would have depressed me because I felt like a corporate drone—and more than once. Each time we were in hunker-down mode, often because of significant budget pressures, it was a time of low energy, low innovation, and low morale. People's unconscious goals were to blend into the woodwork to avoid criticism—or worse. After awhile we just kept behaving like that, even when the budget pressures eased up.

Then, one day, I was at a seminar on leadership effectiveness with about a hundred other people from different organizations, including corporations, family businesses, educational institutions and nonprofits. One of the discussion topics asked us to explore the notion that leading means standing for something, often something larger than ourselves. The seminar leader asked us to come up to the microphone, one by one, and tell the group what we stood for. I was excited by this idea but was dreading going up and making my statement because I had no idea what I was going to say. I was deep in one of my corporate-drone periods, and to be honest, I could only think and speak the corporate line. I felt too exhausted and stressed out to come up with anything particularly personal or enlightening, especially in front of a room full of strangers. Meanwhile, other participants were going up and taking a stand for family values, the needs of the disadvantaged, and the future of education. They were terrific. I felt even more pressure. When it was my turn, I slowly walked up to the microphone, turned and faced the audience, and through the speakers in the ceiling I heard my voice say these words: "My name is Lisa Parker and I am taking a stand to bring humanity back to the workplace." There was a moment of silence, and then everyone started clapping. I blinked a couple of times, taking in both my own words and the audience's reaction. My statement bubbled up from my unconscious, and as I felt the enormous truth of it, I could see that it also resonated with many in the room. After the meeting, people kept coming up to me and telling me how happy they were to hear someone put into words what they'd been feeling themselves. It was a turning point for me, and from that time on, I did my best to interact with people as people. I became much more empathetic and a much better listener, trying to connect with each person on a human level. But most importantly, *I finally let myself be myself at work*, still dedicated, still trying to do my best every day, but with a little compassion for my own humanity. It felt as if this was the last, and best, part of the evolution of the journey I described at the start of Chapter Six.

Why Did I Tell You This Story?

Because you are now going to imagine your own story and make some decisions about your presence as an authentic expression of your true self. In these pages we've consistently encouraged you to be your authentic self. If you were a little too prescriptive in reading this book you might have concluded that you should always walk in a certain way, talk in a certain way, and so forth. You might have concluded that you always have to *be* a certain way. Of course, that's not the intention here at all. In giving you information about the essential elements in Chapter Five, for example, and making you more aware of the impact of stress on presence in Chapter Seven, our goal was to help you understand the myriad of items that can contribute to or detract from your presence, and the impact your behavior can have on how people perceive you and how they respond to you. Our goal is to empower you to be the best you possible and to give you the tools to get there.

Now What?

> *"Tomorrow's illiterate will not be the man who can't read; he will be the man who has not learned how to learn."*
>
> —Alvin Toffler

If you've actively worked your way through part or all of this book and participated in the different activities, you have "learned how to learn"[37] about presence. You probably have a good idea of what you want to work on to strengthen your presence. You may have identified some habitual ways of doing things that helped you in the past but are no longer contributing to your presence in a positive way. You've also taken a step back to consider the context that you work in now, and the importance of managing people's expectations in light of that context.

Your Signature Presence

Each of us is a unique individual. As you make decisions about which aspect of your presence you want to enhance, don't forget the things that make you special, the things that make you *you*. For example, people often comment that I have a lot of energy, which I do. I want to keep that high energy as a part of my signature presence. However, unrelenting high energy can be annoying and might be perceived as "hyper" or "trying too hard." So, I need to keep one hand on the expression-o-meter knob and dial it back when a more mellow style would be more effective.

How about your signature presence? What are the aspects of your personality that people seem to find attractive or special? When you get compliments from people, what do they tend to notice about you? It might be your warmth and smile. It might be your gift for making complex things simple and understandable. It might be the artistic flair in the way you dress. Perhaps it's your gift for making other people feel special or welcome. Maybe you are a superb listener. Or something else?

To begin working on your presence goal, start by reconnecting with your strengths. Take a look at the strengths you listed in Chapter Three. You also might want to review your aspirational adjectives from Chapter Six. Don't lose sight of your known strengths as you work on your presence goal.

Aspects of my signature presence are:

_____

_____

_____

Take a look at what you just wrote down. If you only listed one or two things, perhaps you're not seeing the real you. Keep working. If you wrote four or five things, that's a good strong start. Together, these items should describe you and only you. So, as you read those items in combination, ask yourself: Who else would I use this same group of attributes to describe? If you can think of more than one other person, you haven't identified your unique qualities. Add or change one or two items to get closer to your unique presence elements.

Now, write a positive intention (see page 243) for maintaining these unique qualities:

_____

_____

_____

_____

The positive intention statement is an affirmation of your good, strong qualities. Consider posting that somewhere where you can see it frequently and reinforce it with positive self-talk.

Now let's put together your presence action plan. There is a blank form on page 268. Here are the components:

Presence goal: You may have identified several goals as you worked through this book. Now is the time to choose one (or two at the most) to work on for the next few months. As you review your own notes from the various activities, is there a theme? Do you have a goal that feels especially exciting or relevant to you? To stimulate your thinking, see the list of potential presence goals shown on page 264.

How will it show up? (representative behaviors): Everything we've done in this book is to make something intangible into something tangible. How will your presence goal show up to others? How will you—and they—know that you've taken on this goal?

Benefits of change: What are the benefits for you or your team if you do achieve your presence goal? What might be possible? What sort of result will you need to motivate you to begin in the first place?

Possible first steps: The first step could be something as simple as sharing your goal with trusted colleagues at work, or it might be a little more complicated such as initiating a 360° assessment. Whatever it is, if you know the first step, you can be off to a strong start.

Potential obstacles: We said at the beginning of the book that enhancing your presence is simple but not easy. What might get in the way of you achieving your presence goal? In our seminars, people are often reluctant to admit that the biggest obstacles they face are lack of time and lack of mindfulness. All of our students and coachees are busy professionals juggling many things at once, and they know that the glow of commitment we feel at the end of training or coaching is going to shine for a few days or weeks and then get overshadowed by the demands of the work day. Be honest with yourself about the obstacles. It's okay.

Support needed: What help, guidance, training, or support will you need to push past those obstacles and stay true to your intentional change process? Do you need a coach or mentor to help you focus? Or maybe an automated reminder from your online calendar? Or maybe a class or a book? If you are seeking support from others, how will you engage their support?

Here are some sample action plans:

Sample Presence Action Plan #1

Presence goal: *Be more present with others, especially with my team when they come to my office.*

How will it show up? *(representative behaviors): I'll listen more attentively and allow fewer interruptions from people or my electronic devices.*

Benefits of change: *My team will feel I'm really listening to them, and I might actually learn some new things because I'm doing a better job of paying attention.*

Possible first steps: *Practice at home! I know that I tune out my husband and kids sometimes because I'm checking e-mails on my phone instead of being fully present with them. Also, I'll tell my staff what I'm trying to do and ask them to call me out when they catch me not paying attention.*

Potential obstacles: *It will be hard to break this old habit of hearing my phone beep and going right away to check it. Also, at work, I feel visually distracted when people are in my office because my chair faces the door and hallway.*

Support needed: *I could compromise with my family and only check e-mails at a certain time in the evening. I could get an extra guest chair in my office and sit next to my visitors, which would put my back to the door. I need to remember to turn my phone to silent when I am in meetings. If someone desperately needs something, they know they can call someone else on the team.*

Measures of success: *People will come to me more often and with more enthusiasm. The real measure will be when I am not the least bit distracted by what's going on outside the four walls of my office, and I can stay in the moment.*

Sample Presence Action Plan #2

Presence goal: *Demonstrate more confidence. I feel it, but I don't always show it.*

How will it show up? (representative behaviors): *I will speak up more often and with more volume, and I will be more aware of my posture at meetings and try to sit up a little straighter.*

Benefits of change: *People will actually be able to hear me the first time, so they might not get frustrated with me as often. Also, my ideas and the ideas of my team will be considered more seriously if I can deliver them with more confidence myself.*

Possible first steps: *Do my vocal exercises every day so I know how to produce a louder voice. Before meetings think about how I want to add value and prepare my speaking points in advance. Start my sentences with "I believe" or "In my experience," and so forth. Practice sitting up straighter on the commuter bus and at the dinner table.*

Potential obstacles: *Remembering to sit up straight. I need to get over my self-consciousness when I hear my own voice echo back at me in a room.*

Support needed: *Have my kids remind me to sit up straight. Keep working with my voice coach to strengthen my speaking voice.*

Measures of success: *I would like to get through two weeks in a row without once being asked to repeat myself because someone couldn't hear me. Also, it would be a big win if I heard one of our ideas repeated and praised outside the meeting.*

Now it's your turn. A blank action plan is below. As you choose your goal, remember to go where the energy is.

Your Presence Action Plan

Presence goal:

How will it show up? (representative behaviors):

Benefits of change:

Possible first steps:

Potential obstacles:

Support needed:

Measures of success:

Congratulations! You are the proud owner of your own presence. It's an asset. Take good care of it. Pay attention to it. It has value.

For a complete description of the coaching and classroom services available to our corporate clients, please visit us at **www.HeadsUpCoach.com**.

THE TEN PREMISES

Premise #1: Presence is the sum of one's actions and behaviors.

Premise #2: Behavior can be learned (or relearned) and actions can be managed.

Premise #3: Your career is a collection of moments.

Premise #4: We may not know what presence is, but we know it when we see it.

Premise #5: Leadership is both more personal and more public than ever before.

Premise #6: Objective self-awareness is a pre-condition to being present.

Premise #7: Presence is only "presence" if you are with other people.

Premise #8: All communication is your presence in action.

Premise #9: Being in the moment allows us to adapt quickly and to actively influence what happens next.

Premise #10: Stress is the poison of presence.

HEADS UP PRESENCE MODEL

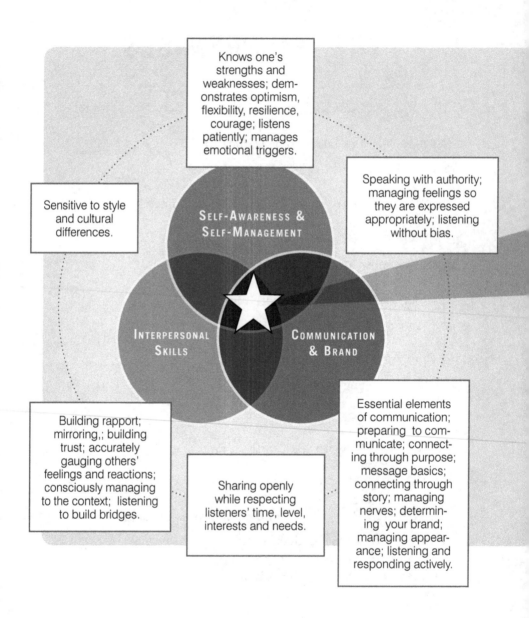

Knows one's strengths and weaknesses; demonstrates optimism, flexibility, resilience, courage; listens patiently; manages emotional triggers.

Speaking with authority; managing feelings so they are expressed appropriately; listening without bias.

Sensitive to style and cultural differences.

SELF-AWARENESS & SELF-MANAGEMENT

INTERPERSONAL SKILLS

COMMUNICATION & BRAND

Building rapport; mirroring,; building trust; accurately gauging others' feelings and reactions; consciously managing to the context; listening to build bridges.

Sharing openly while respecting listeners' time, level, interests and needs.

Essential elements of communication; preparing to communicate; connecting through purpose; message basics; connecting through story; managing nerves; determining your brand; managing appearance; listening and responding actively.

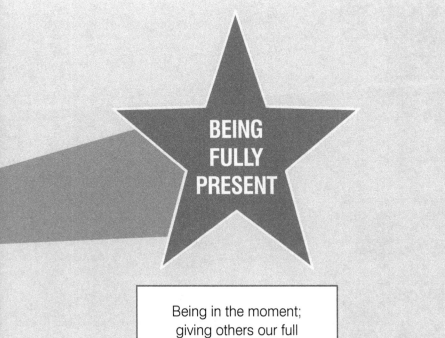

BEING FULLY PRESENT

Being in the moment; giving others our full attention; sharing personal experience to demonstrate understanding; encouraging interaction and collaboration; demonstrating empathy and compassion.

ENDNOTES

1. There is a plethora of good research to support this. Here are two examples: Zenger and Folkman positively correlate leader effectiveness as rated by their 360° feedback scores with employee engagement. John H. Zenger and Joseph Folkman, *The Extraordinary Leader* (New York: McGraw-Hill, 2002). *HBR's* article "Putting the Service-Profit Chain to Work" shows the critical links in the very short chain connecting employee engagement with profitable growth. (Cambridge, MA: Harvard Business School Publishing, March–April 2004).

2. Charles Duhigg, *The Power of Habit: Why We Do What We Do in Life and Business* (New York: Random House, 2012), 89.

3. "Years of neuroscience research have led to the current understanding of the brain as a prediction machine—an amazingly complex organ that processes information to determine what's coming next." David DiSalvo, *What Makes Your Brain Happy and Why You Should Do the Opposite* (Amherst NY: Prometheus Books, 2011), 16.

4. Alan Fine, *You Already Know How to Be Great* (New York: Portfolio Penguin, 2010).

5. Amy Arnsten, "The Mental Sketchpad: Why Thinking Has Limits," lecture delivered at the Neuroleadership Summit, October 29, 2008.

6. Cara Feinberg, "The Mediatrician," *Harvard Magazine* (November–December 2011): 52.

7.   Christine Pearson and Christine Porath, *The Cost of Bad Behavior* (New York: Penguin Books, 2009).

8.   Albert Mehrabian's research is frequently misquoted, suggesting that the percentages apply to all communication. However, Mehrabian is clear that his research was devoted to the hierarchy of attention in mixed messages specifically. Original source: Albert Mehrabian, *Silent Messages* (Belmont, CA: Wadsworth Publishing, 1971).

9.   Although the stigma of crying at work is less now than it was twenty years ago. I was heartened by Alice Andors' interview of Anne Kreamer, author of the new book *It's Always Personal: Emotion in the New Workplace* and quoted in her article "You Can Cry if You Want To," *HR Magazine* (October 2011).

10. There is research that shows that blood pressure increases in both people when one person tries to hide upsetting emotions from another person. From a lecture, "Stay Cool under Pressure," by neuroscientist Kevin Ochsner, delivered at the Neuroleadership Summit, October 29, 2008.

11. Pearson and Porath, 12.

12. Ibid., 13.

13. Daniel Goleman, *Working with Emotional Intelligence* (New York: Bantam Dell, 1998).

14. Remember the research mentioned in Chapter Two that shows that when one person is trying to mask his emotions, the blood pressure for everyone goes up? So much for not getting people upset!

15. Terry Pearce calls this "relevant vulnerability" in his book *Leading Out Loud*. Employees can relate to leaders who share some of the same challenges that they face, and as long as the leader doesn't reveal "crippling vulnerability," people will respond well to leaders who ask for, and give, help when needed. See Terry Pearce, *Leading Out Loud* (San Francisco: Jossey-Bass, 2003), 85–89.

16. Daniel Goleman, 29.

17. Ed Keller and Brad Fay, *The Face-to-Face Book: Why Real Relationships Rule in a Digital Marketplace* (New York: Free Press, 2012), 61.

18. For an excellent explanation of men and their feelings of being put in a "one-up, one-down" position, read Deborah Tannen's *The Power of Talk*, available from HBR Online, Harvard Business School Publishing.

19. Tired of bullet points on slides? Break out of the mold by using any of the books and blogs available today. I recommend Garr Reynolds's book *Presentation Zen* for exciting ideas on using more visual elements (Berkeley, CA: New Riders, 2008).

20. We teach this message model in our seminars all around the world for corporations looking to streamline meetings and increase the impact of presentations. However, there are limits to being able to learn it from a book. For a short white paper on how to create the model using a template, plus an example, please go to our website: www.managingthemomentbook.com.

21. Annette Simmons, *The Story Factor: Secrets of Influence from the Art of Storytelling* (New York: Basic Books, 2006), 5.

22. In her book *Quiet*, Susan Cain describes several research studies that demonstrate the fear of humiliation has a powerful impact on performance. For example, Cain quotes one study by behavioral economist Dan Ariely, which demonstrated that participants solving anagram puzzles alone versus in front of a group performed better. Ariely had predicted the opposite: his hypothesis was that people would perform better in front of an audience because they would be more motivated. But they performed worse. Cain says: "An audience may be rousing, but it's also stressful." Susan Cain, *Quiet: The Power of Introverts in a World That Can't Stop Talking* (New York: Crown Publishers, 2012), 89–90.

23. Three long, slow deep breaths will work wonders in the moments just before you speak, but sometimes you need a little more relaxation. Come to our

website, www.managingthemomentbook.com, for a five-minute, guided, meditation exercise you can use any time you are feeling superstressed.

24. With this technique, do not paraphrase; always use the questioner's exact words unless the questioner uses hostile or emotion-laden words that you do not want to use in your answer.

25. Alison Beard, "Hot or Not," *Harvard Business Review* (October 2011): 144.

26. A terrific book on the relationship between nutrition and energy is Adele Puhn's *The 5 Day Miracle Diet*. The miracle is how high your energy level is after only five days when you eat properly. When you feel great and eventually look fit and healthy, your confidence soars and it shows in your presence. (New York: Ballantine Books, 1996.)

27. Davia Temin, interview by author, New York, 26 March 2012.

28. Daniel Goleman: "EQ and Leadership," video interview with Josh Freedman, YouTube, Fall 2011.

29. Servant leadership is a philosophy and practice of leadership, coined and defined by Robert K. Greenleaf and supported by many other leadership and management writers. Servant-leaders achieve results for their organizations by giving priority attention to the needs of their colleagues and those they serve.

30. Quote is a classic from the original TV show *Lost in Space*, spoken by Robbie the Robot whenever young Will was about to set off on an adventure without realizing the perils.

31. Ronald Heifetz, Alexander Grashow, and Marty Linsky, "Leadership in a (Permanent) Crisis" (*Harvard Business Review*, July–August 2009, 65.)

32. Fey says: "The first rule of improvisation is AGREE. Always agree and SAY YES… which reminds you to respect what your partner has created and to at least start from an open-minded place. Start with a YES and see where that takes you," from Tina Fey, *Bossypants* (New York: Little, Brown, 2012), Kindle edition.

33. Daniel Goleman, *Working with Emotional Intelligence*, 322–323.

34. Ibid.

35. Catalyst, "Women Take Care, Men Take Charge: Stereotyping of U.S. Business Leaders Exposed," available as a free download from their site: www.catalyst.org.

36. Richard Boyatzis and his colleagues have spoken and written extensively on the subject of coaching with compassion and the positive impact on the parasympathetic nervous system. For example, see Richard Boyatzis, "Neuroscience and Leadership: The Promise of Insights," *Ivey Business Journal* (online) (January/February 2011).

37. The quote on page 260 is frequently attributed to Toffler. Toffler himself attributes the origin of the idea to Herbert Gerjuoy.

INDEX

O

optimism, 46, 81–82, 86, 87, 254, 273

other-consciousness, 39, 89, 135, 151, 234

outcomes, 54, 86, 108, 120, 159, 165

overtalking, 99, 165, 181, 246

P

patterns, 24, 31, 40, 42, 93, 95, 114, 141, 175, 204, 234. *See also* data points

Pearson, Christine, 36, 66–67

peer network, 203, 219

perceptions of self, controlling, 206, 208. *See also* branding

performance, 38, 50, 188, 204, 277, 253, 267

      reviews of, 29, 82, 153, 216

Porath, Christine, 36, 66–67

posture, 34, 117, 142, 144, 213,

positive intentions. *See* intentions, positive

PowerPoint. *See* slides

prehistoric ancestors, 90

Premises ("The Ten Premises"), 271

preparation, 93, 151–153, 155–156, 158, 177, 179

presence, 13, 17, 18, 29, 109, 110, 183, 196, 232, 250, 260

      assessment, 238, 253–254, 263

      acquisition of, 14, 18, 24, 28–31

      definition, 23–24, 32–33, 271

      demonstrating, 73, 124, 133, 139, 250

      four behaviors essential to, 85–87

      goals, 39, 262, 264

      managing, 67, 139, 252

      model of, 52–54, 135, 139, 197–198 205, 233, 235, 273

Printed in the USA
CPSIA information can be obtained
at www.ICGtesting.com
JSHW012048140824
68134JS00035B/3325